Westview Replica Editions

This book is a Westview Replica Edition. The concept of Replica Editions is a response to the crisis in academic and informational publishing. Library budgets for books have been severely curtailed; economic pressures on the university presses and the few private publishing companies primarily interested in scholarly manuscripts have severely limited the capacity of the industry to properly serve the academic and research communities. Many manuscripts dealing with important subjects, often representing the highest level of scholarship, are today not economically viable publishing projects. Or, if they are accepted for publication, they are often subject to lead times ranging from one to three years. Scholars are understandably frustrated when they realize that their first-class research cannot be published within a reasonable time frame, if at all.

Westview Replica Editions are our practical solution to the problem. The concept is simple. We accept a manuscript in camera-ready form and move it immediately into the production process. The responsibility for textual and copy editing lies with the author or sponsoring organization. If necessary we will advise the author on proper preparation of footnotes and bibliography. We prefer that the manuscript be typed according to our specifications, though it may be acceptable as typed for a dissertation or prepared in some other clearly organized and readable way. The end result is a book produced by lithography and bound in hard covers. Initial edition sizes range from 400 to 600 copies, and a number of recent Replicas are already in second printings. We include among Westview Replica Editions only works of outstanding scholarly quality or of great informational value, and we will continue to exercise our usual editorial standards and quality control.

Classical Theories of Value:
From Smith to Sraffa
Jeffrey T. Young

This book, an outgrowth of the recent "Cambridge Capital Controversy," presents a new and challenging interpretation of the classical school of economic thought. Jeffrey Young explores the reemergence of the classical theory of value as a significant event in the history of economic thought; in the process, he reveals three characteristic features of classical economic analysis. First, consumer demand is ignored as a primary determinant of value and distribution. Instead, demand is treated as the technically determined maintenance requirement of the economic system. Second, the technically given proportions within the basic sector quantitatively determine relative values, given a rate of surplus value. Thus, the focus on the physical production process clearly distinguishes this approach from the neoclassical, which focuses on the psychological process of evaluation. Third, production is seen as occurring in a historically determined social framework. Hence, institutional data such as social classes are considered prior to and more important than the exchange process. The socially determined distribution of income between wages and profits must be specified in order to determine values; the direction of causation is from technical and social production to exchange.

This view of classical economics leads to three important conclusions. First, the classical school did not disappear around 1870 as is commonly supposed. Instead, this type of economic theory has coexisted with the subjective value approach into the present period. Second, the conventional interpretation of the relation between the classical and the neoclassical theory is wrong. This interpretation, focusing on the continuity between the two, argues that the neoclassical theory constitutes only a refinement and generalization. A more correct interpretation would focus on the substantially different approaches of the two schools, realizing that the emergence of the neoclassical approach is a discontinuity in the history of economics. Third, the classical approach remains relevant because of its broadened subject matter, which now properly includes the social relations of production, and its potential for dealing with long-term growth.

Jeffrey T. Young is assistant professor of economics at Marshall University.

Classical Theories of Value:
From Smith to Sraffa
Jeffrey T. Young

Westview Press **/** Boulder, Colorado

A Westview Replica Edition

Copyright © 1978 by Westview Press, Inc.

Published in 1978 in the United States of America by
   Westview Press, Inc.
   5500 Central Avenue
   Boulder, Colorado 80301
   Frederick A. Praeger, Publisher

Library of Congress Catalog Card Number: 78-19636
ISBN: 0-89158-287-8

Printed and bound in the United States of America

for Cherry

Contents

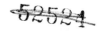

Acknowledgements

Since for all practical purposes this is my doctoral dissertation with some minor revisions, most of which are stylistic, I would like to acknowledge the support given to me by my thesis committee at the University of Colorado at Boulder: Professors Kenneth E. Boulding, George W. Zinke, Suzanne W. Helburn, Ann R. Markusen and Thomas Mayer. From this group I would particularly like to single out Professor Boulding whose support has made this publication possible, and Professor Zinke who first introduced me to the Sraffa analysis and who helped me formulate my interpretation during many enjoyable conversations. In addition I wish to thank Professor Joan Robinson for reading the completed dissertation and providing me with valuable comments.

Naturally, there are many others who have made their own special contribution to this work. Of these I would like to single out Mrs. Barbara Ramey who patiently prepared the typescript.

1. Introduction to the Problem of Value in the History of Economics

> Happily there is nothing in the laws of value which
> remains for the present or any future writer to clear up;
> the theory of the subject is complete...
> John Stuart Mill,
> Principles of Political
> Economy, 1848.

There have been at least two brief periods in the history

of economics when the leading economists have confidently

expressed the triumph of economic science. The first is

evidenced by John Stuart Mill's proclamation above, and the

second by the post war Neoclassical synthesis which proclaimed

the end of the business cycle while maintaining the theoretical

adequacy of the capitalist economy to automatically stabilize

at full employment.[1] The Austrian and Jevonian attack on the

Ricardian theory of value ended the first period of complacency

resulting in the introduction of the marginal utility theory

of value and the subsequent usage of the marginal principle as

the basic mode of analysis in economics. The second period of

complacency has been uprooted by two dissimilar events; the

appearance of simultaneous inflation and recession in advanced

capitalist countries, and less noticeably, the publication of

Piero Sraffa's Production of Commodities by Means of Commodities in 1960.[2] This book has been the mainspring in perhaps the most powerful theoretical challenge yet to the neoclassical orthodoxy of the twentieth century.[3]

SEPARATE TRADITIONS

This second event is the subject of this book. Specifically, we will attempt to place this Sraffian "Revolution"[4] into historical perspective. Since Sraffa's model is widely recognized as an attempt to rehabilitate the older classical economics of Ricardo and Marx, the inquiry is concerned primarily with the classical tradition in economics.[5] As such it is a study of the internal logic of the classical theory of value and its relation to the classical conception of the economy and the economic process. A clear understanding of these connections is presented. Once this is understood it becomes apparent many of the generally accepted interpretations of the development of economic thought are wrong. For example, in future chapters we shall argue that the classical value analysis cannot properly be understood as a special case of the Marshallian supply and demand apparatus, true only in the presence of constant returns, and that, therefore, the classical labor theory is not, strictly speaking, a legitimate forerunner of the modern theory.[6] The history of economic thought must be viewed as characterized by two distinct approaches, both of which have contested the field of economic theory at least from

2

Adam Smith to the present, rather than as a smooth development from classical to neoclassical analysis.

This view of the history of economics gives the classical approach of Ricardo and Marx new relevance since it can no longer be considered the primitive ramblings of dead forerunners. Since the classical approach to value has reappeared in Sraffa and served as a basis for the Cambridge critique of the marginal theory of value and distribution,[7] the historian of economic thought no longer needs to concentrate on minor points of interpretation or on little known forerunners of new ideas. The investigation of Ricardian and Marxian economics can yield insights which can directly influence modern debates and understanding. For example, consider the problem of defining an aggregate quantity of capital. Since neoclassical theory attempts to use this quantity to explain prices and distribution, this aggregate measure must be independent of these quantities.[8] Ricardo faced a similar problem in his system when he attempted to formulate his theory of value and distribution. He wanted a value principle which would not only approximately explain relative prices, but also provide a measure of aggregate social product independent of prices and distribution. This was necessary because he could not have an adequate theory of distribution if the quantity distributed, namely national income, varied with the distribution itself.[9] The modern capital quantity controversy seen in the perspective of Ricardo's problem is a clear example of what Schumpeter is talking about in the following passage:

> teachers or students who attempt to act upon the theory
> that the most recent treatise is all they need will soon
> discover that they are making things unnecessarily dif-
> ficult for themselves. Unless the treatise itself
> presents a minimum of historical aspects, no amount of
> correctness, originality, rigor, or elegance will prevent
> a sense of lacking direction and meaning from spreading
> among the students or at least the majority of students.
> This is because, whatever the field, the problems and
> methods that are in use at any given time embody the
> achievements and carry the scars of work that has been
> done in the past under entirely different conditions. The
> significance and validity of both problems and methods
> cannot be fully grasped without a knowledge of the pre-
> vious problems and methods to which they are the
> (tentative) response.[10]

In attempting an historical analysis of the kind we have
mentioned above, we encounter a difficult problem of interpretation which arises out of our belief that these two schools of
thought are substantially different. As might be expected each
school of thought evolves different ways of writing the history
of economic theory. The nature of schools of thought is such
that they incorporate fundamentally different points of view in
which the questions asked and the abstractions made are different. Consequently different things both in present and in
past theory are emphasized as important. Consequently differences of opinion emerge as to what constitutes good
economics, and differences in evaluating past achievements
logically follow. In a time when conflict is supressed, or
nonexistent, it is often the case that the earlier schools
get pretty rough treatment and are ruled out of court simply
because they are different from the generally accepted modern
theory.[11] As outlined above this is not such a period in the

4

history of economics, and, therefore, an alternative approach is needed which aids rather than hinders meaningful dialogue between the competing schools of thought, both on questions of historical interpretation and on contemporary questions. What is called for is a fundamental type of analysis which uncovers the essence of each point of view by examining the internal logic of the theory. It is assumed the average reader understands the neoclassical theory. Therefore, we concentrate almost exclusively on the classical approach.

THE MEANS TO MEANINGFUL DIALOGUE: COMPARATIVE METHODOLOGY?

Some writers have suggested that the essence of different schools of thought lies in their various methodologies. For example, Lukács has argued Marxism can withstand the total rejection of all the particular theses of Marx, such as the falling rate of profit, because the essence of Marxism is the method of dialetical materialism.[12] Similarly, Joan Robinson states: "A school of thought is distinguished by its methods, not by its tenets."[13] While it is appealing to accept this type of explanation because it seems to offer a way of reducing arguments to basic differences which can then be fruitfully debated, it is still insufficient. Our approach will rely heavily on Schumpeter's concept of "vision" and Kuhn's concept of a "paradigm".[14,15] Schumpeter introduces the concept of "vision" in the History of Economic Analysis thus:

> In practice we all start our own research from the work of our predecessors, that is we hardly ever start

5

from scratch. But suppose we did start from scratch, what are the steps we should have to take? Obviously, in order to be able to posit to ourselves any problems at all, we should first have to visualize a distinct set of coherent phenomena as a worth-while object of our analytical efforts. In other words, analytic effort is of necessity preceded by a preanalytic act that supplies the raw material for the analytic effort. In this book, this preanalytic cognitive act will be called Vision. It is interesting to note that the vision of this kind not only must precede historically the emergence of analytic effort in any field but also may re-enter the history of every established science each time somebody teaches us to see things in a light of which the source is not to be found in the facts, methods, and results of the pre-existing state of the science.[16]

Thus, vision is a broad outline or general perspective associated with each approach to a given reality. In actual analysis it manifests itself in the basic theoretical categories, variables, and methodology. We will consider it the essence of a school of thought, and it will be our primary concern to look at classical economics and then to elaborate its vision or world view as applied to the economic process. As Schumpeter indicates this type of inquiry is particularly important during an historical period when new ideas, or old ideas in modern form (Sraffa), attempt to sway professional opinion away from traditional modes of thought. Economics is currently in such a period and has been for much of its history.

Kuhn's concept of a "paradigm" helps to more fully elaborate this train of thought. In the history of any science there eventually comes a period of development when diverse, disjointed inquiry begins to emerge into a relatively clearly defined model which tends to unify thought and scientific

6

practice. According to Kuhn, this unifying model becomes a paradigm.[17] It is the most basic product of the vision which underlies it. A model, or a particular scientific achievement, is a paradigm if it "defines the legitimate problems and methods of a research field for succeeding generations of practitioners," while at the same time leaving unanswered all sorts of questions for future researchers to solve using the basic theoretical structure of the original achievement.[18] It is a primitive expression of a school of thought.

Two features of a paradigm are worth nothing. First, as previously noted, paradigms do not answer all the questions which are considered essential for scientific understanding. Rather, they provide a framework for development. Followers of a given school of thought do not assert their approach has solved all problems of understanding. Rather, they choose to follow a particular approach because they have faith this analysis is fundamentally correct and will, therefore, serve as a framework within which the problems will eventually be solved. This suggests it is invalid to object to a particular school on the grounds that everything is not explained. Rather objections must be clearly aimed against the paradigm itself on the grounds that the basic vision precludes important questions "because they are not objects of this theory, because they are forbidden by it."[19] Second, by focusing the inquiry of the scientific community, paradigms define the set of questions and puzzles which are subjected to intensive investigation,

7

and they tend to influence the observer's perception because they indicate what should be there to see, and, hence, create blindness to objects and events whose existence is anomalous to the paradigm. Objects and events which lie outside this field of vision are not looked upon as objects worth studying or events in need of explanation until a new paradigm comes along with a new vision which incorporates these anomalies, and thus, challenges the original view. Indeed, as Althusser has pointed out

> [Science] can only pose problems on the terrain and within the horizon of a definite theoretical structure, its problematic, which constitutes its absolute and definite condition of possibility, and hence the absolute deter-mination of the forms in which all problems must be posed, at any given moment in the science.[20]

Thus, since existing theoretical models fundamentally structure our observation, they also determine the meaningfulness and the specific content of the questions asked. Hence, meaningful discourse between adherents of different paradigms, based on different visions, is extremely rare.

It is our contention that this type of discourse is not only desirable on the abstract level of the pursuit of "Truth"; it is absolutely essential for a much more important reason. In the preceding section we talked abstractedly about the close interrelation between perception and the basic theoretical model used to organize that which is perceived. However, visions and paradigms in economics have not developed histor-ically as abstract exercises in pure logic. They have developed within a social milieu in which the economist takes an active role, i.e., he develops theory in order to support policy pronouncements on the crucial social issues of the times.[21] There has always been a close correlation between theoretical economics and social values. Consider for example, Zinke's discussion of Malthus:

> Being objectively observable, moral and social values can be taken into account by any social theorist, and he can substitute certain ones among them for his own prepossessions or modify the latter in the light of his scholarly investigations. For what these will or may disclose is that certain ideas of value, which originally he does not personally entertain, do make a difference to others--and enough difference to enough others to recommend themselves for his acceptance in the place of his original preferences, or in modification of the latter. Therefore, to state that considerations of social and moral values entered into Malthus' theorizing in a determining fashion is not at all the equivalent of saying that his personal predispositions governed his scholarly and civic endeavors. To that significant extent to which Malthus made appeal to observable value-facts of life, he contributed important social knowledge which others could find worthy of consideration even though not all of them chose to act on it after examining it. That is the most any social scientist can strive to accomplish.[22]

Since economic theory plays this type of social role, it is essential to achieve dialogue on the fundamentals so that reason can be used to resolve value conflicts. If, on the contrary, the basic underlying value conflicts are considered irrelevant to progress in economics, then objective reason is excluded from the social decision making process which must confront actual value differences.

If debate in economics, such as the capital controversies, were conducted with this in mind, the disputants would feel responsible to get at the basic visions or world views of the different positions. Opinions on what is good or bad, just or unjust, etc. are closely linked to a vision of the way the social system is actually constructed. This vision is capable of being clarified and stated logically such that reason can be applied to test validity. Hence, vision is the key to applying scientific reason to values conflicts. In this study we will attempt to illuminate the vision of the classical tradition so that dialogue can begin on this fundamental level. It is our hope that this exercise will bring the historical role of economics as a branch of the study of human values back into the forefront of economic thought.

To conclude, the overriding importance of vision means methodology alone is insufficient to get at the essence of schools of thought. The method of investigation is itself a product of the particular vision of the investigator. For example, Marx's method is frequently described as dialectical materialism,[23] but Marx did not come upon this ready-made for his use, nor did he develop it in complete isolation from the events and objects he was investigating. Since he viewed human societies as essentially developmental, dynamic systems, he considered the dialectic the only correct method for perceiving in thought this type of reality. Since he perceived that human behavior tended to "fit in" with the requirements of the material conditions of production, he considered materialism the correct approach to comprehending the parallelism

10

of ideas and the mode of production. His methodology, far from

being distinct from his specific ideas, is itself a product of

his basic vision of the outlines and patterns in human society.

THE MEANS TO DIALOGUE: THE THEORY OF VALUE

In economics the theory of value has formed the unifying

theoretical achievement which has organized inquiry in different

schools of thought. It is the foundation of economic inquiry.

> Value is the essence of things in economics. Its laws are
> to political economy what the law of gravity is to
> mechanics. Every great system of political economy up
> till now has formulated its own peculiar view on value as
> the ultimate foundation in theory of its applications to
> practical life, and no new effort at reform can have laid
> an adequate foundation for these applications if it cannot
> support them on a new and more perfect theory of value.[24]

The theory of value gains its importance in economics because

historically it has constituted the

> unifying quantitative principle which enabled [Political
> Economy] to make postulates in terms of the general
> equilibrium of the economic system--to make deterministic
> statements about the relationships which held between the
> major elements of the system.[25]

Any paradigm in economics will be characterized by a theory of

value which reveals the basic model around which inquiry on

other subjects is structured. For example, the classical

paradigm only really took shape after Adam Smith's theory of

natural price systematized many diverse writings on the problems

of money and exchange. Once this breakthrough occurred a whole

series of puzzles occupied the best economic thinkers for

several generations. In particular, the determination of the

natural prices of land, labor, and capital was central to the

11

classical theory of distribution, and the great debates which
flourished on the relative roles of supply and demand versus
labor time in the determination of prices received their impetus
from Smith's theory and from his inability to give a definitive
explanation of their determination.[26]

Since value theory occupies such a central place in
economics, we might logically expect an in-depth study of a
school's theory of value to lead us to the underlying vision
which is characteristic of that school. Indeed, Meek argues:

> When an economist sets out to analyze the economic process
> he generally starts with a kind of 'vision' . . . of that
> process. This 'vision" normally includes some sort of
> basic principle of causation which the economist decides
> will be useful in the explanation process, and this
> principle of causation tends to find expression in the
> theory of value [emphasis added] with which his subsequent
> analysis begins. The theory of value expresses in a
> generalised way the angle from which the economist
> believes the process should be analysed.[27]

Our investigation will, therefore, involve a survey of the
development of the classical theory of value from the early
labor theories of Smith, Ricardo, and Marx to the modern
commodity theory of Sraffa followed by a more detailed discussion of the vision which underlies and is common to both.

Since we are placing such strong emphasis on the theory of
value, a more specific discussion of the role of value theory
is in order. In his 1937 essay, "The Requirements of a Theory
of Value," Dobb elaborates on this theme.[28] In its formal
aspects any economic theory can be stated as a system of
simultaneous equations which represents a simplified, abstracted

12

model of a given reality. For formal adequacy the number of equations must equal the number of unknown quantities so that the system is capable of solution.[29] In addition, a solution of the unknowns requires knowledge about certain constants or values which are known independently of the other variables in the system.

> For instance, the "gravitational constant" which figures in the Newtonian physics expresses the acceleration of a body as (in part) a function of mass; and is valid in so far as one can treat mass as something independent of velocity. If, however, (as more recent concepts are suggesting), the mass of a body in turn varies with its velocity, this constant is to that extent inadequate as a basis for calculating changes in velocity.[30]

In economics these constants are provided by the theory of value, e.g. hours of labor time in Ricardo and Marx. Thus, the first formal requirement of a theory of value is to provide the crucial constant so that the system of general statements about reality is capable of solution.

These systems of equational statements are necessarily abstractions from a complex reality. Therefore, the theory of value will only allow solutions which approximate an actual situation. This is a fact of life in any science and, there-fore, criticisms leveled against the abstract and approximate nature of a theory of value tend to miss the mark.[31] The important thing is not that abstractions have been made, but that our approximate solutions give a good understanding of those events which we care about.[32] In other words, we do not abstract from important aspects of reality. Thus, the second

13

formal requirement of a theory of value is that it allows us to make reasonably close approximations of those important features of reality.

The particular principle we choose for our theory of value depends partly upon the degree of generality toward which we are striving. "The more particular, and less general, the problem to hand, the greater number of surrounding conditions which one is justified in assuming constant."[33] For example, when dealing with the price of a particular commodity on a given day all one needs to know is the quantity of the good available on that day and something about the strength of peoples' desires for the good along with some information about budget constraints and the price policy of the seller. Here it is legitimate to assume wages, rents, and profits are constant since they will not influence the market period price. However, as one generalizes to longer periods and more commodities, it is no longer permissible to assume these factor payments are constant since changes in their level will influence prices and vice versa.[34] Thus, the third requirement of a theory of value is to provide a principle to determine these factor payments as well as commodity values. It must be simultaneously a theory of value and distribution. To express this more succinctly, the theory of value "must express a relationship with some quantity which is not itself a value."[35] This is why simple cost of production theories, such as Adam Smith's, and supply and demand theories have only limited validity

14

without some principle such as utility or labor time expressing the ultimate forces lying behind price phenomena.

Perhaps the most obvious outward feature of value in the real world is that it is a quantitative relation. The price of a shirt expresses a relation between numbers of shirts and numbers of dollars. Hence, a primary goal of economic theory is to make quantitative statements about the relationships between the variables which enter the analysis. This gives us the fourth formal requirement. The value principle must be formulated such that it allows us to express these abstract statements in terms of quantitative entities in the actual system. But, this is not sufficient for the purpose of making quantitative statements. The value principle must also give us a rule to reduce the diverse entities which enter price to a common term.[36] This illuminates the weakness of those theories of value which have attempted to explain price in terms of labor and abstinence. Without any rule for establishing a functional relationship between the quantity of labor and the quantity of abstinence it is impossible to make quantitative statements about price. This is the old problem of adding apples and oranges. It cannot be done without expressing them in common units.

> This seems to provide the reason why the two major value-
> theories which have contested the economic field have
> sought to rest their structure on a quantity which lay
> outside the system of price-variables, and independent of
> them: in the one case an objective element in productive
> activity, in the other case a subjective factor underlying
> consumption and demand.[37]

15

We are now in a position to sum up Dobb's argument. For formal
adequacy a theory of value must allow us to explain actual price
phenomena on the basis of some entity, such as labor or utility,
which is not itself a value, and which reduces the diverse
elements of price to a common term, such that we are able to
make approximate, quantitative statements which allow us to
understand the development of that slice of reality we have
isolated as being of primary importance. These requirements
alone are sufficient to critique simple cost of production
theories, such as Adam Smith's adding-up theory, and "real cost"
theories, such as Senior's labor plus abstinence theory. The
former is inadequate because it relates value phenomena to
quantities which are themselves values, hence it is open to the
charge of circularity if it is used in a context broader than
market period phenomena. The latter is invalid because it
provides no rule for determining the relation between labor
and abstinence, even if abstinence itself could be quantified.
We are left with the classical labor theory of value and the
neoclassical subjective theory as the two theories which appear
to satisfy the above criteria. Both attempt to provide a set
of independent determining constants which give content and
meaning to a purely formal system of simultaneous equations.

From Dobb's analysis it should now be clear that an
adequate theory of value makes the difference between a theory
which gives a reasonable approximation to reality and supports
the conclusions we wish to draw and a theory which does not.

Therefore, we can now see more clearly that the theory of value
is the keystone in a system of economic thought. It provides
the link between a purely formal set of equations, which on
their own are devoid of real content, and the actual economic
system we are studying. It provides substance and meaning.

Our analysis in the coming chapters will proceed as
follows: Chapter 2 will elaborate the classical/Marxian tradition, concentrating on the development of the labor theory of
value motivated by the need to construct a consistent standard
of value and the need to explain adequately the effect of the
rate of profits on values. Chapter 3 will begin our analysis
of Sraffa by presenting the fundamentals of his commodity
theory of value. We will then have an overview of the classical theory which we will analyze in more detail in Chapter 4
which describes the classical vision of the economic process.
The argument developed is that despite the clear differences
between Sraffa and the earlier classics, they both are based on
a similar conception of value arising out of the interface
between the physical requirements of production and the particular form of social production relations in a capitalist
economy. Chapter 5 will then look broadly at the whole
development of economic thought, trying to develop a basic
framework in which a more complete history of economic thought
might be written. We will look at some of the conventional
interpretations of the relation between classical and neoclassical economics, and we will argue that the appearance of

17

Sraffa and the subsequent debates mean the classical tradition has not been totally abandoned and replaced by the modern theory of value and distribution. Consequently the history of economic thought needs substantial rewriting to clearly bring to the fore the internal logic of, the development of, and the conflict between two distinct paradigms. A dual approach is needed to capture this complexity. Finally, we will include a brief section on where theoretical and practical research might be directed to use Sraffa's higly abstract apparatus to return economic thought to the social role of economics as an aid to desirable social change.

NOTES

1. While this may strike one as being a bold statement, it seems, nevertheless, to capture the flavor of Samuelson's pronouncement that "If Marxians wait for capitalism to collapse in a final crisis, they wait in vain." Paul A. Samuelson, Economics, 8th ed. (New York: McGraw-Hill Book Company, 1970), p. 250. See also, Hyman P. Minsky, John Maynard Keynes, (New York: Columbia University Press, 1975), pp. 49-54.

2. Piero Sraffa, Production of Commodities by Means of Commodities, (Cambridge: Cambridge University Press, 1960).

3. We use the term "neoclassical" to refer to the school of thought in economics which uses the marginal principle in conjunction with a subjective theory of value in analyzing the problem of price and distribution as market processes divorced from the institutional arrangements of the social system.

4. P. R. Brahamananda, The New-Classical Versus the Neo-Classical Economics, (Mysor: Prasaranga University of Mysore, 1967).

5. Ronald L. Meek, "The Rehabilitation of Classical Economics," reprinted in Economics and Ideology and Other Essays, (London: Chapman and Hall, Ltd., 1967), p. 161.

6. This interpretation goes back to Alfrad Marshall, Principles of Economics, 8th ed., (New York: Macmillan Co., 1948), p. 814.

7. For an in-depth survey of the Cambridge capital controversies see Geoffrey C. Harcourt, Some Cambridge Controversies in the Theory of Capital, (Cambridge: Cambridge University Press, 1972).

8. Ibid., pp. 11-46.

9. Maurice Dobb, Theories of Value and Distribution Since Adam Smith: Ideology and Economic Theory, (Cambridge: Cambridge University Press, 1973), p. 84.

10. Joseph A. Schumpeter, History of Economic Analysis, (New York: Oxford University Press, 1968), p. 4.

11. An example of this type of argument can be found in Frank Knight's "The Ricardian Theory of Production and Distribution," in The Canadian Journal of Economics and Political Science 1 (1, 2, 1935): 3-25, 171-196. By accusing Ricardo of failing to

recognize production is the creation of services, not the creation of things, and by failing to study Ricardo in terms of his own theoretical problematic, Knight essentially argues Ricardo is wrong because he differs from the neoclassical approach which is assumed to be correct.

12. George Lukács, History and Class Consciousness, new ed., (Cambridge Massachusetts: MIT Press, 1971), p. 1.

13. Joan Robinson, "Marxism: Religion and Science," Collected Economic Papers, Vol. 2, (Oxford: Basil Blackwell, 1964), p. 155.

14. Schumpeter, History of Economic Analysis, pp. 41ff.

15. Thomas S. Kuhn, The Structure of Scientific Revolutions, 2nd ed., (Chicago: The University of Chicago Press, 1970), p. 10ff.

16. Schumpeter, History of Economic Analysis, p. 41.

17. Kuhn, Scientific Revolutions, p. 10.

18. Ibid., p. 10.

19. Louis Althusser and Etienne Balibar, Reading Capital, (New York: Pantheon Books, 1970), p. 26.

20. Ibid., p. 25.

21. This is the central theme of Leo Rogin's The Meaning and Validity of Economic Theory, (New York: Harper and Brothers, 1956).

22. George W. Zinke, The Problem of Malthus: Must Progress End in Overpopulation?, University of Colorado Studies/Series in Economics, No. 5, (Boulder: University of Colorado Press, 1967), p. 64.

23. Lukács, History and Class Consciousness, p. 1.

24. Friedrich von Wieser, Natural Value, (New York: Kelley and Millman, 1956), p. xxx, cf. Schumpeter, p. 588.

25. Maurice Dobb, "The Requirements of a Theory of Value," in Political Economy and Capitalism, Some Essays in Economic Tradition, (London: Routledge & Kegan Paul, Ltd., 1972), p. 5.

26. The most famous of these debates is, of course, the Malthus-Ricardo debates on a number of issues, including the theory of value. These can be found in their entirety in Piero

Sraffa ed., The Works and Correspondence of David Ricardo (Cambridge: Cambridge University Press, 1951). For a discussion on the underlying social values see Zinke, p. 77.

27. Ronald Meek, Studies in the Labour Theory of Value, 2nd ed., (London: Lawrence and Wishart, 1973), p. 129.

28. Dobb, Political Economy and Capitalism, pp. 1-33.

29. Ibid., p. 5.

30. Ibid., p. 7.

31. Criticisms of the labor theory of value based on the problems arising from unequal capital/labor ratios tend to fall into this category. If Ricardo's theory of distribution or Marx's laws of development of capitalism are essentially unchanged when the theory is made more general, then the simple labor principle is sufficient for the purpose at hand.

32. Dobb, Political Economy and Capitalism, p. 8.

33. Ibid., p. 8.

34. Ibid., p. 9.

35. Ibid., p. 10.

36. Ibid., p. 11.

37. Ibid., p. 12.

2. The Development of the Classical Tradition in the Nineteenth Century

In attempting to understand classical economics we are immediately confronted with the existence of two traditions in economics, because adherence to a school of thought also affects the interpretation of alternative schools and the progress of ideas in general. Consider the following statements about Ricardo's theory of value:

> I can find no basis for the belief that Ricardo had an <u>analytical</u> labor theory of value, for quantities of labor are not the determinants of relative values. Such a theory would have to reduce all obstacles to production to expenditures of labor or assert the irrelevance or non-existence of non-labor obstacles...[1]

> Thus the secondary effect of unequal proportions of capital, far from qualifying and weakening the anti-Smith corollary of his primary value principle, served to reinforce it with something of the effect of a paradox. It was hardly surprising in the circumstances that he should have treated his primary cause (quantity of labour) as being 'never superseded' by the 'second cause' (variations in capital proportions and durability) 'but only modified by it.'[2]

These two passages are indicative of these traditions. One, typified by Stigler, holds that Ricardo for all practical purposes abandoned the labor theory of value in favor of a cost of production theory of value in the tradition of Smith and

Marshall. This tradition views the early history of economic thought from the perspective of modern neoclassical theory. The other, typified by Dobb, argues that Ricardo never abandoned this basic value analysis, and, therefore, he is more properly placed as a forerunner of Marx than Marshall. This tradition attempts to maintain a distinction between early classical and modern neoclassical theory by looking at classical economics in terms of its own problematic. Hence, the existence of these two alternatives, the classical and the neoclassical, gives rise to a split in understanding the historical development of economics. The basic vision of a school of thought extends to the problems of historical interpretation. The neoclassical tendency to view classical economics as a primitive form of neoclassical theory, Ronald Meek has called the teleological approach to the history of thought.[3] Little attempt is made to understand the past on its own grounds within its own perception of the world and the problems to be solved by economic analysis. Prior to Keynes this view might have appeared as legitimate, especially in the wake of Marshall's integration of classical cost concepts with the subjective theory of value. However, this approach breaks down in the face of the re-emergence of the classical theory. Its role in the critique of neoclassical theory clearly reveals the weakness of the teleological approach, because this approach implies a broad consistency between the two schools.

In this study we will consciously attempt to understand

23

classical economics on its own ground, carefully avoiding the
temptation to fall into the teleological interpretation.[4] We
will rely on the original works of Smith, Ricardo, Marx,
Dmitriev, Bortkiewicz, and Sraffa in conjunction with commentators such as Dobb, Meek, and Sraffa who work within this
tradition to present our discussion of the development of the
classical theory.

ADAM SMITH

Adam Smith is particularly difficult to summarize coher-
ently on the theory of value partly because there are problems
in his terminology and partly because he develops modes of
analysis associated with classical theory and modes of analysis
typical of neoclassical theory. In a real sense he is the
fountain head of both. Nevertheless we shall do our best,
concentrating on his contributions to the classical tradition.
Smith begins his value analysis with the famous paradox of
value:

> The word VALUE, it is to be observed, has two different
> meanings, and sometimes expresses the utility of some
> particular object, and sometimes the power of purchasing
> other goods which the possession of the object conveys.
> The one may be called 'value in use;' the other 'value in
> exchange.' The things which have the greatest value in
> use have frequently little or no value in exchange; and
> on the contrary, those which have the greatest value in
> exchange have frequently little or no value in use.[5]

From here he develops in Chapter 5 his famous labor command
theory which is based on the notion of labor as "the ultimate
and real standard by which the value of all commodities can at

24

all times and places be estimated and compared. It is their real price..."[6] Then Chapter 6 makes the first reference to a labor embodied principle and lays out wages, rent, and profit as the components of price, while Chapter 7 brings out the distinction between market price and natural price. From here the analysis looks for the determination of the natural rates of wages, rent, and profit. This is all very familiar ground which does not need further elaboration.

The primary source of confusion on Smith is that in the first book of the Wealth of Nations he has put forth at least four theories of value; a labor command theory, a labor embodied theory, a disutility of work theory, and a cost of production theory. He immediately rejects the labor embodied theory because it only applies to the "early and rude state of society" where all the product goes to labor. He then takes up a cost of production-theory which he carries through the rest of the analysis. Thus, if we must assign one theory of value to Smith, it would have to be a cost of production or adding-up, theory since the bulk of his value analysis is devoted to an analysis of the forces which determine the component parts of price. According to Meek, Smith developed this type of analysis instead of a labor embodied theory because of his earlier insistence that labor command was the true value of commodities.[7] Whereas in the "early and rude state" labor command and labor embodied would be equal in equilibrium, this would not in general be true in a society where there was a

25

class of landlords receiving rent and a class of capitalists receiving profit, since these forms of income are paid out of the natural price of a commodity but represent no labor embodied. In this type of situation the two measures of value yield identical results if wages constitute a constant proportion of the total value of all commodities.[8] However, in a society where there has been some capital accumulation, this will not generally be the case. Hence, Adam Smith opted for the cost of production theory. He, therefore, sought the explanation of the quantitative aspects of value in the forces which regulate the equilibrium rates of wages, rent, and profits, apparently in the belief these were independent determinants.[9]

Smith has made four major contributions to the development of a classical tradition. First and foremost he seems to be among the first to clearly distinguish the outlines of capitalist society as a distinct mode of subsistence which were so important for Ricardo and Marx. He perceived the division of society into workers, capitalists, and landlords as the basis of economic analysis.[10] This comes out clearly in the discussion above of his rejection of the labor embodied principle. Along these same lines he was also the first to recognize the existence of a separate class of capitalists who gained profit as a distinct income. Moreover, this profit income tended to arise from the employment of wage labor, and tended to equalize as a percentage of the capital advanced regardless of the particular industry in which the capital was employed.[11] Profit and its analysis became the central problematic of the classical theory of value.

Second, Adam Smith clearly distinguishes between market price, as the day-to-day price of a good on the market determined by the available supply and the effective demand, and the natural price which represents the price toward which the market price tends in the long run. As did later classicists, Smith considered the determination of natural price the primary problem of the theory of value.

Third, Smith focuses his value analysis on the supply side of the market. His adding-up theory of price is a cost theory which is an important step in the development of the classical labor theory of value because it focuses on the long run tendencies of wages and profits to establish an equilibrium rate, and, more importantly because it considers demand to be essentially unrelated to the problem of value perceived as the laws which determine the natural price of commodities. In particular, demand in Smith's analysis determines the extent of the division of labor, the amount of each commodity produced, and market price in conjunction with available supply, but it does not affect natural price.[12]

Fourth, Smith opened up the long discussion which so troubled Ricardo on the appropriate measure of value. He clearly understood the problem of making comparisons between different nations and different times, and he attempted to

27

develop a measure which would be applicable to all times and places in that it would register a change in the true value of a commodity only when there was a change within the production requirements of that commodity such that the amount of labor for which it could exchange changed. Thus, since labor was conceived as invariant, the concept of absolute value has meaning in Smith's analysis because a change in the amount of labor commanded in exchange would indicate that only the real value of the commodity changed in spite of the fact that the relative value of both the commodity and labor changed.[13]

DAVID RICARDO

Since the publication of Sraffa's introduction to the Works and Correspondence of David Ricardo any complete analysis of Ricardo's theory of value starts with his theory of profits.[14] In his "Essay on Profits" Ricardo makes the assertion that the general rate of profits is governed by the rate of profit in agriculture.[15] The rate of profit in agriculture is determined in a simple corn model by the relation between corn used as capital, which forms the subsistence fund for labor, and corn output. In this simple model corn is the only commodity and labor is the only input to the production process. The corn-rate of profit is determined by the capacity of agricultural labor to produce more than what is needed for subsistence. As Sraffa noted:

> The rational foundation of the principle of the deter-
> mining role of the profits of agriculture, which is never

28

explicitly stated by Ricardo, is that in agriculture
the same commodity, namely corn, forms both the capital...
and the product; so that the determination of profit by
the difference between total product and capital advanced,
and also the determination of the ratio of this profit to
the capital, is done directly between quantities of corn
without any question of valuation. It is obvious that
only one trade can be in the special position of not
employing the products of other trades while all the
others must employ its product as capital. It follows
that if there is to be a uniform rate of profits in all
trades it is the exchangeable values of the products of
other trades relatively to their own capitals (i.e.
relatively to corn) that must be adjusted so as to yield
the same profit as has been established in the growing of
corn; since in the latter no value changes can alter the
ratio of product to capital, both consisting of the same
commodity.[16]

Sraffa then goes on to argue that the advantage of this approach

lies in its enabling us to determine the rate of profit with-

out reducing a heterogeneous collection of capital goods to a

common standard.[17] In other words profits are determined by a

purely physical relation without reference to the problem of

value.[18]

In order to defend his proposition about the rate of

profit in agriculture, Ricardo had to move from his original,

simple corn model to a more general model in which many

commodities were produced and many commodities entered the

subsistence basket of the workers. In order to do this he

needed a theory of value. He, therefore, developed his labor

theory of value to serve two primary functions. First, he

needed an independently determined quantity which would allow

him to reduce heterogeneous goods to a common standard so that

a ratio between capital and net product could be calculated in terms of this common standard so that the rate of profits would still reflect the physical relation between capital goods and output. Second, he needed a theory of value to show how the prices of other commodities adjusted to changes in the conditions of production in the wage goods industry.[19]

We are now in a position to look at the labor theory of value Ricardo expounded in the Principles in the light of the specific problems he is trying to confront with it. The analysis begins with the typical distinction between exchange value and use value, and with the conclusion that "Utility . . . is not the measure of exchangeable value."[20] Thus, at the outset the analysis focuses on the production process, and in particular those

> commodities only as can be increased in quantity by the exertion of human industry, and on the production of which competition operates without restraint.[21]

Ricardo then goes on to accept a labor embodied approach to value in opposition to Smith's labor command on the grounds that the two are rarely equal and that the labor embodied approach gives a standard of value which "is under many circumstances an invariable standard, indicating correctly the variations of other things" while the quantity of labor which a commodity can command in exchange is highly variable.[22] Having determined the quantity of labor as the basis and cause of exchange value, Ricardo then brings in a second cause of value which modifies the original statement. This is the effect of wages on value in circumstances where the durability of

fixed capital and the quantity of fixed capital combined with
labor varies in different lines of production.

> This difference in the degree of durability of fixed
> capital, and this variety in the proportions in which the
> two sorts of capital may be combined, introduce another
> cause, besides the greater or less quantity of labour
> necessary to produce commodities, for the variations in
> their relative value--this cause is the rise or fall in
> the value of labour.[23]

The reason this is true is because capital must earn the going
annual rate of profit for each year it is invested. The product
of ten hours of labor employed over two years must receive a
higher price than the product of ten hours of labor employed
for only one year.

This admission of a second cause of value is frequently
cited as proof Ricardo never held a labor theory of value, but
rather he held a cost of production theory in the tradition of
Adam Smith before him and Mill and Marshall after his death.[24]
However, as Dobb has recently pointed out Ricardo himself
regarded this second cause of value in no way to be a concession to Smith's component parts of price analysis of natural
price.[25] To realize this we must first understand Ricardo
developed his theory as a critique of Smith explicitly to
refute the notion that the price of corn governs all prices in
the sense that a rise in the price of corn would cause a rise
in all prices.[26] In fact, by admitting the effect of wages on
value, Ricardo was able to strengthen his refutation of Smith.
Smith had claimed the price of corn regulates all prices; a
rise in its value would cause all prices to rise. This is a

direct corollary of the adding-up theory since corn is the wage good. In Ricardo's analysis an increase in the value of labor would not cause all values to rise. On the contrary, the value of commodities produced with relatively more fixed capital would fall relative to other commodites.[27] If we keep in mind that Ricardo's theory of value was developed in order to substantiate his simple corn theory of profit in a more general model, we can see clearly why the second cause of value strengthened his theory instead of weakening it. As Sraffa has observed:

> The 'principle problem in Political Economy' was in his view the division of the national product between classes and in the course of that investigation he was troubled by the fact that the size of this product appears to change when this division changes . . .
>
> Thus the problem of value which interested Ricardo was how to find a measure of value which would be invariant to changes in the division of the product; for, if a rise of wages by itself brought about a change in the magnitude of the social product, it would be hard to determine accurately the effect on profits.[28]

Ricardo clearly saw that a satisfactory theory of value had to be grounded in some quantity or relation which was independent of other values in order to avoid the circularity involved in determining value by other values.

However, he was never able to construct an analytically complete theory of value which determined relative prices and the correct standard of value when fixed capital varied in its durability and in the proportions in which it combined with labor. The best he could do was delineate the conditions which an invariable standard would have to meet. These are contained in the unfinished essay "On Exchangeable Value and

32

Absolute Value," which Ricardo worked on during the last weeks of his life in 1823.[29] First, a satisfactory standard of value must have value and that value must be invariable.[30] Second, in order to be invariable the commodity must be produced with an average proportion of fixed capital and labor.[31] Ricardo admitted he was unable to discover any commodity in reality which would meet the second criterion, although he did assert nature has provided labor as a "standard . . . by which we can ascertain the uniformity in the value of a measure."[32] Later in the essay he suggests using labor employed for one year as the standard to measure absolute value.[33]

Since Ricardo was unable to find a commodity which could serve as a standard in which to express value, we must conclude he was unable to solve satisfactorily the problems posed by his approach to value. However, this did not stop him from using his theory to formulate his model of distribution. For the purposes of developing practical conclusions Ricardo felt justified in using a simplified value analysis.[34] This was the simple labor quantity theory in which value was determined by the relative quantity of labor embodied in commodities. In terms of our previous discussion of the theory of profits, corn as input is replaced by the value of the subsistence goods consumed by workers, and corn as output is replaced by the value of the goods produced by labor at the margin in the wage goods sector which was assumed to be agriculture. Thus, the rate of profit is determined by the ratio of the value of net output to

33

the value of input.[35] From here Ricardo was able to develop his theory of the falling rate of profit which served as the basis of his indictment of the Corn Laws. Profits would fall as the margin of cultivation was pushed to increasingly inferior land because the value of labor would rise relatively to the value of other goods forcing down profits.[36]

This concludes our discussion of Ricardo's theory of value. Although his work is confusing on distinguishing the cause of value from the measure of value,[37] he made improvements of fundamental importance such as his insistence on explaining value on the basis of expenditure of human labor time rather than on the expenditure of wages[38] and his recognition of the problems, caused by fixed capital, in explaining relative natural prices and in deriving a standard of value. In particular, he was the first to formulate a theory of value which satisfied the formal requirements discussed in Chapter 1 above. He isolated the quantity of labor measured in hours as the independent, determining constant which allowed him to construct a determinate model from which he derives corollaries and predictions concerning the actual economic system. Certainly Adam Smith was able to achieve a sufficiently accurate and consistent theory of value to support his analysis of the relation between the individual and the public interest. However, Ricardo's was the first economic model which was tightly constructed, and he was the first to understand the necessity of explaining value in terms of something which is

34

not itself a value. Furthermore, he developed the labor theory of value to show profit arose from the existence of a value difference (which reflected the physical fact of surplus production) between the product of labor and the subsistence of the laborer. The theory of value was the center piece of the Ricardian system.[39]

KARL MARX

Although Marx's interest is much broader than Ricardo's as his early writing on social alienation points out, he inherited the body of analysis as developed by Ricardo, and used its basic propositions as a starting point for his own economic analysis. This proceeded along two major fronts. First, Marx attempted to understand the mechanism within capitalist society which produced the value difference mentioned above and caused the surplus to accrue to the class of owners rather than the class of producers. To Marx this value difference appeared as an unequal exchange between capitalist and worker which was implicit in Ricardo but which Ricardo never perceived.[40] Second, Marx placed his analysis within his general theory of history. In so doing he attempted to correct what he perceived as the fundamental weakness of the classical analysis; namely

> it had an historical, eternal, fixed and abstract conception of the economic categories of capitalism. Marx says in so many words that these categories must be historicized to reveal and understand their nature, their relativity and transitivity. The Classical Economists, he says, have made the conditions of capitalist production

35

the eternal conditions of all production, without seeing that these categories were historically determined, and hence historical and transitory.[41]

Thus, Marx's dialectical-materialist conception of history is perhaps the central focus of his analysis of economic value and the major improvement on his classical forerunners. It should, therefore, come as no surprise that this conception dominated his theory of value. His conception of history was that history must be understood as a succession of different modes of production wherein each mode is characterized by different forms of human productive activitv using different instruments of labor and by different forms of social relations within the production process. Marx's general method approaches the study of society from the point of view of the social production process and the social relations within this process.

> It was natural that an historical conception of this kind, when applied to a particular economic system, should approach the matter from the angle of conditions of production, including socio-economic factors as ownership of means of production and the respective effects of these upon the situation and behavior of social groups or classes.[42]

This desire to relate economic phenomena such as exchange and value to the productive process and relations is clearly evident in Marx's value analysis. In Chapter 1 of Capital Marx presents the heart of his value analysis.[43] Value first appears as exchange value. In this stage of development exchange value appears as an entirely accidental relation existing on the fringes of society. There is not yet developed

36

any uniformity or custom which serves to regulate exchange value quantitatively.

> Hence exchange-value appears to be something accidental and purely relative, and consequently an intrinsic value, i.e. an exchange-value that is inseparably connected with, inherent in commodities, seems a contradiction in terms.[44]

This is the case of exchange considered as a peripheral social phenomenon. However, when the division of labor develops sufficiently, exchange becomes a daily necessity. This is what Marx called commodity society.[45] In this type of society exchange value no longer is an accidental relationship, but rather is a fully developed, determinate relationship. It thus becomes the intermediary between people. Each person performs a task which is socially useful and exchanges his product for those of others which he needs. Value has a "purely social reality" in the sense that it only emerges in a commodity society as the social bond. Individuals in this society receive the power of exchanging for their subsistence because they have contributed labor to the common pool of labor producing the necessities of society.[46]

Value is, therefore, a social relation which manifests itself in a relation between commodities.[47] Because value appears as a relation between things its essence is obscured. Consequently, most economic thought has not penetrated behind exchange and the world of commodities to the social relations which lie behind them.

> A commodity is therefore a mysterious thing, simply because in it the social character of men's labour appears

37

to them as an objective character stamped upon the product of that labour; because the relation of the producers to the sum total of their own labour is presented to them as a social relation, existing not between themselves, but between the products of their labour. This is the reason why products of labour become commodities, social things whose qualities are at the same time perceptible and imperceptible by the senses.[48]

This habit of thought, which does not see human productive activity carried on in a social environment as the ultimate source of value, and, therefore, attaches independent existence to commodities by explaining value on the basis of certain properties of the commodities themselves, Marx calls the fetishism of commodities.[49] Rubin has argued this idea is central to Marx's theory of value. This is because the notion of value as a social relation between people reflected in the exchange relation between commodities is the major corollary of looking at commodity society from the point of view of the production process and production relations dominating the development of society. This means Marx

rejected theories which derived value from use value, money from the technical properties of gold, and capital from the technical productivity of the means of production. Economic categories, (or social forms of things) are of course very closely related to the material process of production, but they cannot be derived from it directly, but only by means of an indirect link: the production relations among people.[50]

Hence the doctrine of fetishism is central to Marx's criticism of other theories, and in the development of his own.

The discussion thus far has focused entirely on the qualitative value problem which attempts to explain the nature of value. However, value is both a qualitative and a quantitative relation.[51] Marx was also interested in deriving quantitative statements from his theory of value. In particular he was interested in analyzing the unequal exchange between the capitalist and the workers. We will now turn to Marx's quantitative value analysis. Here we will only be concerned with his specific improvements over Ricardo's labor embodied theory.

Both Marx and Ricardo argued relative long run equilibrium prices were determined by the relative quantity of labor expended including the previous labor congealed in fixed capital. However, they differed on their definitions of value. For Ricardo value was natural price, but for Marx value was labor embodied. Ricardo argued value was determined by labor embodied while Marx argued relative prices were determined by value.[52] Thus, in Marx's analysis value becomes an unseen force operating behind the scenes. Specifically in Marx's theory, value is created by abstract human labor which to Marx is a real, although hidden entity. In commodity society where exchange is a highly developed, regularized social process the act of exchange explicitly equalizes different use values and implicitly equalizes the different types of concrete useful labor which created the use values.[53] Since this is done regularly and since labor is free to flow from one employment to another, it made sense to Marx to think of society as possessing a pool of labor which could be used to create any use value society desired. Marx considered this pool social labor in the abstract, because the concrete ways it could be used

39

were not limited by the particular current uses of the labor.
It was the social fact of exchange which causes any individual
laborer to expend both useful labor creating articles of use
for society and abstract labor, creating exchange value.
Abstract labor is an innovation of Marx's which is tied in
closely with his understanding of commodity society and the
nature of the social relations which produce exchange value as
a specific historical category.[54]

In terms of the quantitative problem Marx made two major
improvements. First, in analyzing the exchange between capitalist and laborer, Marx made the value difference between
subsistence and output central to his theory of profit. The
specific innovation which allowed Marx to develop the theory of
surplus value was the concept of labor power. In the Preface
to Volume II, Engels discusses why classical political economy
failed to perceive the source of the value difference, and how
Marx's concept of labor power makes the problem remarkably easy:

> Labour is the measure of value. However, living labour in
> its exchange with capital has a lower value than mate-
> rialized labour for which it exchanged. Wages, the value
> of a definite quantity of living labour, are always less
> than the value of the product begotten by this same
> quantity of living labour or in which this quantity is
> embodied. The question is indeed insoluble, if put in
> this form. It has been correctly formulated by Marx and
> thereby answered. It is not labour which has a value.
> As an activity which creates values it can no more have
> any special value than gravity can have any special
> weight, heat any special temperature, electricity any
> special strength or current. It is not labour which is
> bought and sold as a commodity, but labour-power. As
> soon as labour-power becomes a commodity, its value is
> determined by the labour embodied in this commodity as a
> social product. This value is equal to the labour socially

> necessary for the production and reproduction of the commodity. Hence the purchase and sale of labor-power on the basis of its value thus defined does not at all contradict the economic laws of value.[55]

The concept of labor-power enabled Marx to understand the origin of surplus value as a value difference. Ricardo, as we observed above, perceived the value difference, however, it remained a mystery to him and his followers because it appeared that the value of labor changed in the production process.[56] Since input and output were measured in terms of labor, and since output exceeded input it appeared the value of labor had increased during production. In Marx the value difference is clearly perceived as the difference between the value of labor-power and the value of the products of labor. This was completely in line with the laws of competitive markets that on the average equal values are exchanged.

Marx's second contribution is probably more important for the present study. He was the first classical economist to recognize the labor theory of value as a regulator of the total social production process, i.e. he began to perceive the economy from the general equilibrium of the inputs and the outputs as a whole. "The law of value is the law of equilibrium of the commodity economy."[57] Marx perceives the law of value as more than an abstract statement about the relation between exchange value and abstract human labor.[58] The law of value is the regulator of commodity production. Exchange at labor values insures general equilibrium of the input/output structure of

41

the economy. If, as Marx believed, the mix of final products
dictates a certain mix of input products because of technical
relationships, then in an unplanned economy there must be some
mechanism to insure the production of these inputs in the
proper proportions. This mechanism is the law of value which
distributes the social labor force to the branches of production in the correct proportions.

> It requires a fully developed production of commodities
> before, from accumulated experience along, the scientific
> conviction springs up, that all the different kinds of
> private labor, which are carried on independently of each
> other, and yet as spontaneously developed branches of the
> social division of labour, are continuously being reduced
> to the quantitative proportions in which society requires
> them. And why? Because, in the midst of all the acciden-
> tal and ever fluctuating exchange-relations between the
> products, the labour-time socially necessary for their
> production forcibly asserts itself like an over-riding
> law of Nature. The law of gravity thus asserts itself
> when a house falls about our ears.[58]

Consider the following model of simple reproduction. Following
Marx's notation,

Let

c = value of constant capital used in production,
v = value of labor power (variable capital) expended,
s = surplus value produced by variable capital.

Assume the economy consists of two departments. One (I)
produces means of production (c) and the other (II) produces
subsistence and luxury goods (v + s), then if

$$I \quad 4000_c + 1000_v + 1000_s = 6000_c$$
$$II \quad 2000_c + 500_v + 500_s = 3000_{v+s}$$

equilibrium requires sector I to exchange 2000 value units of
means of production for 2000 value units of articles of

consumption. Therefore, the proportions of variable and constant capital enforce an echange ratio of 1/1, which is identical to the labor embodied ratios.[60]

However, as Ricardo had previously noted the market system will establish natural prices proportionate to labor embodied ratios only if the ratio of constant to variable capital is equal in both departments. This is because the competitive market tends to equalize rates of profit on capital in all branches of production. In the example above the ratio of labor values which would equilibrate the exchange between the two departments would have produced unequal rates of profit if the ratio c/v had been different in the two branches.[61,62] Marx, of course, was well aware of the problem and made the first attempt to solve the problem by showing how to transform labor values into competitive equilibrium prices, or prices of production. This is the famous transformation problem which has been a major source of debate within the Marxist school and between the Marxist and non-Marxist economists. As we shall see in the next chapter a viable theory can be constructed from classical roots without the transformation problem appearing. Nevertheless, it is significant as a transition from Marx's schemes of reproduction to Sraffa's production equations. First, Sraffa's analysis clearly developed in response to the same set of theoretical problems which Bortkiewicz, Winternitz and others have dealt with in their consideration of the transformation problem.[63] Second, consideration of the problem

43

explicitly introduced the general equilibrium framework which
had always been implicit in the notion of indirect labor. However, it is important to emphasize the Sraffa system circumvents
some specific aspects of the problem such as the relation
between the sum of values and the sum of prices of production
on the one hand and the sum of surplus value and profits on
the other. This is a consequence of setting up the system as
a price of production model from the outset and showing its
consistency with reduction to dated labor. Also Bortkiewicz's
path-breaking solution of the problem noted the work of
V. K. Dimitriev, a Russian mathematical economist, who
approached the problem from a similar angle as Sraffa. Therefore, we will use these brief points as a rationale for treating Dimitriev's work as an important forerunner of Sraffa which
relieves us of the duty of undertaking an extensive journey
into the mathematics of the transformation problem. The
important point is Marx's attempt to solve the problem and his
schemes of reproduction constitute the transition in the history
of the classical tradition from partial analysis to a general
equilibrium model in which prices and profits are simultaneously
determined.[64]

This concludes our discussion of Marx's value analysis.
As has been sufficiently noted he made several important
contributions to the classical tradition. He placed his theory
within a broad perspective which clearly expressed value as an
historical category based on certain social relations of

44

production. As a result he developed the concept of abstract labor, and argued that the direction of causation was from production relations to exchange relations. He elaborated on Ricardo's theory of profit by introducing the concept of labor power distinct from labor itself. Lastly, and perhaps most importantly, he began to perceive the economic system as a whole and attempted to produce a value theory of general equilibrium in order to solve the problem of unequal proportions of means of production and labor which so troubled Ricardo.

V. K. DMITRIEV

V. K. Dmitriev (1868-1913) is a little known Russian mathematical economist. He concerns us here because he has made an important contribution to the development of the classical tradition. Althought not a classicist himself, he had a clearer understanding of the logical structure of the Ricardian theory of value than any of his contemporaries.[65] His specific merit lies in his success in laying down for the first time the mathematical structure of Smith's and Ricardo's theory of value based on systems of production equations.[66] These equations provide a vital link to Sraffa's production equations of the modern period.

Let

$$X_A = \text{price of product A,}$$

$n_A, n_1, n_2, \ldots, n_m$ = number of working days expended, directly and indirectly, in the production of A,

a = amount of the wage good consumed by workers in a day,

X_a = price of the wage good,

$y_A, y_1, y_2, \ldots, y_m$ = total profits incorporated in A,

then the cost of production and price of A is given by:

$$X_A = (n_A a X_a + n_1 a X_a + n_2 a X_a + \ldots + n_m a X_a) + y_A$$

$$\tag{1}$$

$$+ y_1 + y_2 \ldots + y_m.$$

Now if we replace total profits by rates of profit earned on capital in each branch of production entering the production of A we have

$$X_A = n_A a X_a (1 + r_A)^{tA} + n_1 a X_a (1 + r_{K1})^{tK1}(1 + r_A)^{tA} +$$

$$\tag{2}$$

$$n_2 a X_a (1 + r_{K2})^{tK2}(1 + r_{K1})^{tK1}(1 + r_a)^{tA} + \ldots,$$

where tA, tK1, tK2, are the time periods in which labor is expended directly on A and indirectly on capital types 1 and 2 in the production of A, and r_A, r_{K1}, r_{K2}, are the rates of profit earned in sectors A, K1, K2. Defining a similar production cost equation for B we can determine the price of A in terms of B as:

$$\frac{X_A}{X_B} = \frac{n_A a X_a (1 + r)^{tA} + n_1 a X_a (1 + r)^{tA1} + n_2 a X_a (1 + r)^{tA2} + \ldots}{m_B a X_a (1 + r)^{tB} + m_1 a X_a (1 + r)^{tB1} + m_2 a X_a (1 + r)^{tB2} + \ldots}$$

$$\tag{3}$$

where we now have a uniform rate of profit and where tA1 = tA + tK1 is the time period from investment in capital type 1 until product A is sold on the market, and similarly for tA2, tB1, tB2. Now since , n_A, n_1, n_2, . . . ; m_B, m_1, m_2, . . . ; tA, tA1, tA2, tB, tB1, tB2, . . . ; a, are given by the technical requirements of production, X_A/X_B would be known as a function of these requirements if the rate of profit were known.

> It is to Ricardo's credit that he was the first to note that there is one production equation by means of which we may determine the magnitude of r directly (i.e. without having recourse for assistance to the other equations). This equation gives us the production conditions of the product a to which in the final analysis the expenditure in all products A, B, C, . . . is reduced.[67]

This product, a, is the wage good, and its production equation is given by:

$$X_a = aX_a[N_a(1 + r)^{ta} + N_1(1 + r)^{tal} + . . .$$

$$+ N_q(1 + r)^{taq}],$$

(4)

Where N_a, N_1, . . . , N_q are defined analogously to n_A, n_1, . . . , n_m above.

Dividing by X_a and rearranging terms gives:

$$0 = a[N_a(1 + r)^{ta} + N_1(1 + r)^{tal} + . . .$$

$$+ N_q(1 + r)^{taq}] - 1.$$

(5)

From (5) the rate of profit can be determined from the conditions of production without reference to prices. Thus, $r = f(N_a, N_1, . . . , N_q; ta, tal, ta2, . . . , taq; a)$ all of which are given exogenously by the conditions of production and the social subsistence of the worker. By providing the

the first rigorous and correct theory of production price, Dmitriev has also shown that the classical theory is not guilty of arguing in a circle as Walras and others have argued they did.[68]

This concludes our discussion of pre-Sraffa writings in the classical school. We have made no attempt as yet to define classical economics nor to look at the elements which are basic to a classical approach. This will be done in the fourth chapter. However, accepting the conventional wisdom which asserts Smith, Ricardo, and Marx are classical economists, we have presented an overview of the classical theory of value concentrating on the specific changes and improvements which were made from Smith to Dmitriev. In terms of development it seems the tendency has been to develop the theory into a general equilibrium model, based on the technical input/output structure, which simultaneously determines prices and profits. Therefore, it is necessary to present the classical general equilibrium model as conceived by Sraffa, and then to use our overview of the classical school to look at the basic features of the analysis which makes both the earlier labor theory of value and the later general theory of production price essentially classical.

NOTES

1. George J. Stigler, "Ricardo and the 93% Labor Theory of Value," in Essays in the History of Economics, (Chicago: University of Chicago Press, 1965), p. 333.

2. Maurice Dobb, Theories of Value and Distribution, p. 81.

3. Ronald Meek, "The Decline of Ricardian Economics in England," Economica 17 (65, 1950): 43.

4. In terms of the two passages quoted above it should now be clear that Stigler is guilty of the teleological view since he attempts to understand Ricardo's value analysis from the point of view of neoclassical analysis, never confronting the issue as to whether his perception of the requirements of a sound value theory are the same as Ricardo's. Dobb, however, cannot be accused of this mistake because he is operating within the classical tradition, and is therefore approaching the problem on the grounds laid out by Ricardo himself.

5. Adam Smith, An Inquiry into the Nature and Causes of the Wealth of Nations, edited by Edwin Cannan, (New York: Random House, Inc., 1937).

6. Ibid., p. 33. What Smith is getting at in this discussion is the problem of index numbers rather than the determination of actual exchange values. However, his insistence on labor as the true value of all commodities sheds light on his ultimate acceptance of a cost of production rather than a labor embodied theory of value.

7. Ronald Meek, Studies in the Labour Theory of Value, pp. 70-71.

8. Dobb, Theories of Value and Distribution, p. 49.

9. Meek, Studies in the Labour Theory of Value, p. 71.

10. Ronald Meek, "Adam Smith and the Classical Theory of Profit, in Economics and Ideology and Other Essays, p. 18.

11. Ibid., p. 19.

12. Meek, Studies in the Labour Theory of Value, pp. 73-74.

13. Dobb, Theories of Value and Distribution, p. 48.

14. Piero Sraffa, Introduction to the Works and Correspondence of David Ricardo, (Cambridge: Cambridge University Press, 1951), p. xxi.

15. David Ricardo, "Essay on the Influence of a Low Price of Corn on the Profits of Stock," Works and Correspondence, Vol. 4, pp. 12-13.

16. Sraffa, p. xxi. This interpretation of Ricardo seems to have become the generally accepted view in England. Since the appearance of Sraffa's "Introduction," Meek, Kaldor, Dobb, Robinson, and Eatwell have all incorporated the idea of a commodity which is its own means of production into their discussions of Ricardo. It should also be pointed out that this theory of profits based on the productivity of labor in agriculture clearly denies those interpreters who claim Ricardo treated profit as an unexplained residue. An example of this can be found in J. M. Clark's article "Distribution," in American Economic Association, Readings in the Theory of Income Distribution, (Philadelphia: Blakiston, 1946), p. 61.

17. Sraffa, p. xxxii.

18. Although the physical ratio is sufficient to determine the rate of profit, it is wrong to conclude profit is therefore, a purely technical or "natural" category of income. As a category of income it exists by virtue of a particular form of social relationships and institutions.

19. Dobb, Theories of Value and Distribution, p. 73.

20. David Ricardo, Principles of Political Economy and Taxation, (London: J. M. Dent & Sons, Ltd.), p. 5. Ricardo seems confused here between the measure and cause of value. Although these are distinct problems they are closely related in Ricardo's mind since the problem of a measure is solved if there exists a commodity whose value is invariant to changes in distribution, a cause of variation in other commodities. (See Dobb, Theories of Value and Distribution, p. 82.)

21. Ricardo, Principles, p. 6.

22. Ibid., p. 7.

23. Ibid., p. 18.

24. Examples of this interpretation are not hard to find among neoclassical historians of economic thought. Cf. Stigler; Mark Blaug, Economic Theory in Retrospect, (Homewood, Illinois: Richard D. Irwin, Inc., Revised Edition, 1968), p. 96; and J. M. Cassels, "A Re-interpretation of Ricardo on Value," Quarterly Journal of Economics, 49 (2, 1935): 518-532, and Marshall, Principles of Economics, pp. 813-821.

25. Dobb, Theories of Value and Distribution, p. 76.

26. Ibid., p. 80.

27. Ibid., p. 80.

28. Sraffa, pp. xlviii-xlix.

29. David Ricardo, "Note on Absolute Value and Exchangeable Value," Works and Correspondence, Vol. 4, pp. 357-412.

30. Ibid., p. 361.

31. Ibid., p. 372.

32. Ibid., p. 381.

33. Ibid., p. 405.

34. One of the many places where Ricardo gives his rationale for using the simplified analysis is in the "Notes on Malthus," where he states: "I have myself stated that in proportion as fixed capital was used; as that fixed capital was of a durable character; and in proportion to the time which must elapse before commodities can be brought to market, the general principle of the value of commodities being regulated by the quantity of labour necessary to their production, was modified; but I was of the opinion, and still am of the opinion, that in the relative variation of commodities, any other cause, but that of the quantity of labour required for production, was comparatively of very slight effect." (David Ricardo, "Notes on Malthus," Works and Correspondence, Vol. 2, pp. 58-59.)

35. Sraffa, p. xxxii.

36. Dobb, Theories of Value and Distribution, pp. 74-75.

37. Meek, Studies in the Labour Theory of Value, pp. 123-124.

38. Meek, "Decline of Ricardian Economics," p. 53.

39. Ibid., p. 47.

40. Meek, Studies in the Labour Theory of Value, pp. 123-124. Also Althusser, Reading Capital, p. 23.

41. Althusser, pp. 91-92.

42. Dobb, Theories of Value and Distribution, pp. 144-145.

43. Karl Marx, Capital, Vol. 1, (Moscow: Progress Publishers), pp. 43-87.

44. Ibid., p. 44.

45. See, for example, Marx's explanation in chapter one of the fetishism of commodities where he states, "articles of utility become commodities, only because they are products of the labour of private individuals or groups of individuals who carry on their work independently of each other." (Marx, pp. 76-77.)

46. Ibid., p. 54.

47. Isaak Illich Rubin, Essays on Marx's Theory of Value, (Detroit: Black and Red, 1972), p. 34.

48. Marx, Vol. 1, p. 77.

49. Ibid., pp. 76-87.

50. Rubin, Marx's Theory of Value, p. 41.

51. Paul M. Sweexy, The Theory of Capitalist Development: Principles of Marxian Political Economy, (New York: Monthly Review Press, 1942), pp. 23-56.

52. Meek, Studies in the Labour Theory of Value, p. 209, and Schumpeter, History of Economic Analysis, p. 596.

53. Marx, Vol. 1, p. 57.

54. Cf. Rubin, Marx's Theory of Value, pp. 71, 134, and Meek, Studies in the Labour Theory of Value, p. 165.

55. Frederick Engels, Preface to Capital, Vol. 2, p. 18.

56. Althusser has an interesting discussion of this problem of understanding Marx's criticism and improvement in the classical analysis of surplus. See Althusser, Reading Capital, p. 22 ff.

57. Rubin, Marx's Theory of Value p. 67. Although the Physiocrats had earlier discovered the idea of technical interdependence determining a general equilibrium, they did not express this with a theory of value, an essential element in any discussion of a commodity society.

58. This tends to refute the argument of Joan Robinson and Schumpeter that Marx's theory is purely metaphysical. While there may be metaphysical aspects to his analysis, this aspect

of the law of value based on technical interdependencies in production is not metaphysical. (Joan Robinson, Economic Philosophy, Garden City, New York, Doubleday, Inc., 1964, pp. 35-47, and Schumpeter, p. 596.

59. Marx, Vol. 1, pp. 79-80.

60. Marx, Vol. 2, pp. 401-406.

61. For example consider the following:

$$\text{I} \quad 60_c + 20_v + 10_s = 90_c \quad (c/v = 3)$$
$$\text{II} \quad 30_c + 30_v + 15_s = 75_{vts} \quad (c/v = 1).$$

Labor values which establish equilibrium are 1/1, but they will not obtain in a competitive market since the rates of profit, $s/(c + v)$, are 1/8 in department I and 1/4 in department II. Market equilibrium is inconsistent with labor embodied values.

62. Marx calls c/v the organic composition of capital. It is interesting to note Marx's definition: "The composition of capital is to be understood in a two-fold sense. On the side of value, it is determined by the proportion in which it is divided into constant capital or value of the means of production, and variable capital or value of labour-power, the sum total of wages. On the side of material, as it functions in the process of production, all capital is divided into means of production and living labour-power. This latter composition is determined by the relation between the mass of the means of production employed, on the one hand, and the mass of the labour necessary for their employment on the other. I call the former the value-composition, the latter the technical composition of capital. Between the two there is a strict correlation. To express this, I call the value-composition of capital, insofar as it is determined by its technical composition and mirrors the changes of the latter, the organic composition of capital." (Marx, Vol. 1, p. 574). Apparently Marx felt he had to differentiate value composition from organic composition because in the general case the value composition will change with changes in the rate of profit. Since he wanted an exact correspondence with the technical composition, he introduced the concept of the organic composition. This is precisely Ricardo's problem with a standard of value. Contrary to those who consider this unimportant to his theory, he was well aware of the problem, and took steps to avoid it.

63. Bortkiewicz, L. von, "Value and Price in the Marxian System" reprinted in International Economic Papers 2 (1952): 5-60. Winternitz, J., "Values and Prices: A Solution to the So-Called Transformation Problem," Economic Journal, 58 (1948): pp. 276-280. Meek, R., "A Plain Person's Guide to the

Transformation Problem," in Smith, Marx and After," (London: Chapman and Hall, 1977), pp. 95-119.

64. Ronald Meek, "Value in the History of Economic Thought," History of Political Economy 6 (3, 1974): 246-260.

65. In fact Dmitriev's understanding of Ricardo was only equalled by Marx until Sraffa's Introduction was published in 1951.

66. Domenico M. Nuti, ed., V. K. Dmitriev: Economic Essays on Value, Competition and Utility, (Cambridge : Cambridge University Press, 1974), pp. 39-95.

67. Ibid., p. 59.

68. Ibid., pp. 51-52. Leon Walras, Elements of Pure Economics, 4th ed., (London: Allen & Unwin, Ltd., 1954), pp. 424-425.

3. Sraffa's Theory of Value

In 1960 Piero Sraffa published a very significant and controversial book entitled Production of Commodities by Means of Commodities,[1] which some recognized as a re-emergence of the classical theory value and distribution.[2] As such it deserves a prominent place in our discussion of the development of classical economics. Clearly Sraffa's work is critical in the general development of our basic argument. We want to use it to help uncover the essence of classical theory in order to argue this necessitates a reinterpretation of the history of value theory as a simultaneous development of two distinct paradigms. Therefore it is necessary to give a more complete summary of the essential features of his model. Once we have done this we will then look briefly at the comments given by his reviewers. This will give us a number of ideas on the relation between Sraffa and the early classical writers discussed above. It will also provide a number of insights into the crucial differences between the classical theory and the more conventional neoclassical theory.

Sraffa's model is critical for two reasons. First, as the most advanced treatise in the classical tradition it gives us

important insights into the nature of that tradition which are
not immediately evident from the earlier writings. Second, it
provides a new perspective on the history of economic thought
which insists not only on making a clear distinction between
classical and neoclassical theory, but also that neoclassical
economics is not a logical extension of classical theory.
These ideas will be developed more fully in the last two
chapters.

We must now turn to the basic Sraffa model. Suppose we
have a subsistence economy which produces only wheat and iron.
Suppose further that both commodities are used to produce wheat
and both are used to produce iron and that the proportions used
are given by the existing methods of production. Then, we
might have a production system which is characterized by the
following relations:

280qr wheat + 12t iron → 400qr wheat

120qr wheat + 8t iron → 20t iron.

This system will be in a self replacing state if wheat workers
exchange 120qr of wheat for 12t of iron, i.e. if the exchange
ratio is set at 1 ton of iron for 10 quarters of wheat. These
would be equilibrium prices since they would insure the
replacement of the original means of production and thus allow
the process to repeat itself ad infinitum. These "values
spring directly from the methods of production."[3] This simple
example can be expanded to any number of commodities.

Let

a, b, . . . , k be k different commodities
        A = the annual output of commodity a,
        B = the annual output of commodity b,

. . . .

        K = the annual output of commodity K,
$A_a, B_a, \ldots, K_a$ = quantities of a, b, . . . , k
                annually used to produce A,
        P_a = price of a,
        P_b = price of b, etc.,

then the production equations are given in value terms by:

$$A_a P_a + B_a P_b + \ldots + K_a P_k = A P_a$$
$$A_b P_a + B_b P_b + \ldots + K_b P_k = B P_b$$

. . . .

$$A_k P_a + B_k P_b + \ldots + K_k P_k = K P_k$$

where

$$A_a + A_b + \ldots + A_k = A;$$

$$B_a + B_b + \ldots + B_k = B;$$

and

$$K_a + K_b + \ldots + K_k = K.$$

Since we have stipulated that the total output of each commodity exactly equals the total amount of that commodity used as means of production, one of the structural equations is redundant, i.e. any one equation can be deduced from the others. Hence we have k - 1 independent equations. If we allow one commodity to serve as the standard of value and set its price equal to one, we have k - 1 prices and a determinate system for prices.

This is no longer the case when we add a surplus above subsistence to the system. With the existence of surplus it is

no longer possible to deduce the kth equation from the others
since the equalities specified above between the amounts used
as means of production and the amounts produced of each commodity no longer obtain. In general the total produced will now
be greater than the total used as means of production.

The distribution of the surplus between the different
branches of production must be determined at the same time as
prices and through the same mechanism. This is because the
surplus cannot be allotted before prices since it accrues as
profit to each sector calculated as a percentage of the capital
advanced, and this cannot be computed as a ratio between
heterogeneous goods without reference to their prices.
Conversely, the surplus cannot be allotted after prices are
determined because prices cannot be determined in the first
place without knowing the rate of profit. Therefore, a
simultaneous solution is called for.

The production equations with a uniform rate of profit
(r) in each branch are now given by:

$$(A_a P_a + B_a P_b + \ldots + K_a P_k)(1 + r) = AP_a$$
$$(A_b P_a + B_b P_b + \ldots + K_b P_k)(1 + r) = BP_b$$
$$\cdots\cdots\cdots\cdots\cdots\cdots\cdots\cdots\cdots\cdots\cdots$$
$$(A_k P_a + B_k P_b + \ldots + K_k P_k)(1 + r) = KP_k$$

where

$$A_a + A_b + \ldots + A_k \leq A$$
$$B_a + B_b + \ldots + B_k \leq B$$
$$K_a + K_b + \ldots + K_k \leq k.$$

We now have k equations since, with the introduction of surplus, the equality conditions are no longer generally valid. If, as before, we allow any one commodity to serve as the standard of value, setting it equal to unity, we shall have only $k - 1$ unknowns. However, we can take "r", the rate of profits as a variable, whose value is determined by the system as a whole. Thus, this system is once again determinate.[4] The introduction of surplus brings in a concept which is central to Sraffa's analysis. This is the concept of a basic versus a luxury commodity. A basic is a commodity which enters into the production of all other commodities including its own. A luxury is a commodity which does not enter into the production of other commodities. The importance of this distinction is that luxury items play no role in the determination of prices and profit. This is because removing the production equation of such a non-basic commodity completely removes its price from the system since, by hypothesis, it does not act as the means of production elsewhere in the system. We are left with one less equation and one less price. The other prices and the rate of profit are still determinate.

This distinction is also important in understanding a crucial point about the difference between Sraffa's conception of value and the traditional supply and demand theory. When speaking of basic commodities ideas such as cost of production are to be avoided because they imply a separation between the demand side of the price relation and the supply side which is

59

meaningful only if they are independent. With a basic commodity supply and demand are not independent since, "Its exchange ratio depends as much on the use that is made of it in production of other basic commodities as on the extent to which those commodities enter its own production."[5] Therefore, Sraffa deliberately avoids the terminology of the supply and demand theory in favor of the terms "value" and "price" used in the same sense as the older classical usage to mean natural price or price of production.[6]

In order to generalize the model, Sraffa introduces wages as a share in the net product. This introduces the idea that wages are composed of a subsistence component which is given and a surplus component which is variable. As a concession to the orthodox treatment Sraffa decides to assume the entire wage is variable. Wages thus enter the Sraffa system as a portion of the surplus product which is distributed to labor after production has been completed.

Let

L_a, L_b, . . . , L_k = the annual proportion of the labor force employed in the production of A, B, . . . , K, so that
$L_a + L_b + . . . , + L_k = 1$,
w = the wage per unit of labor,

then the production equations become:

$$(A_a P_a + B_a P_b + . . . + K_a P_k)(1 + r) + L_a w = AP_a$$
$$(A_b P_a + B_b P_b + . . . + K_b P_k)(1 + r) + L_b w = BP_b$$
$$. . . . .$$
$$(A_k P_a + B_k P_b + . . . + K_k P_k)(1 + r) + L_k w = KP_k$$

where

$$A_a + A_b + \ldots + A_k \leq A$$
$$B_a + B_b + \ldots + B_k \leq B$$
$$\cdots\cdots\cdots\cdots\cdots\cdots$$
$$K_a + K_b + \ldots + K_k \leq K$$

The portion of the total output which remains after the replacement of means of production is the national income. This is a composite commodity which can be used as the standard for expressing the value magnitudes wages, profits, and prices. If we set the value of this composite commodity equal to unity we have another equation:

$$[A - (A_a + A_b + \ldots + A_k)] \; P_a + [B - (B_a + B_b + \ldots + B_k)]$$
$$P_b + \ldots + [K - (K_a + K_b + \ldots + K_k)] \; P_k = 1.$$

This gives the system $k + 1$ equations and $k + 2$ unknowns, because w and r are both variables. The system now has one degree of freedom in the sense that wages or profit must first be fixed to make the system determinate.

This brings us to a problem which is familiar from our earlier discussion of the classical theory of value. This is the problem of differing proportions of labor to the means of production. If we have the special case where $\underline{r} = 0$ and $\underline{w} = 1$, relative values will be in proportion to the relative quantities of direct and indirect labor used in production. This is well known. However, once we allow $\underline{w}$ to fall and $\underline{r}$ to rise from this initial position the key to the movement of relative prices lies in the proportions in which labor and the means of

61

production enter the production process of the different industries, i.e. these proportions will determine the relative impacts of a rising r on the price equations given above. As is also generally known, relative values will not be affected if these proportions are equal in all industries. Since in general this is not the case, we can expect industries with less than the average amount of labor relative to means of production to show a deficit when w falls as r rises. The fall of w does not generate enough revenue to pay the higher rate of profit. Conversely, we can expect industries with more labor relative to the means of production than the average to show a surplus. The fall of wages generates more than enough revenue to pay the added profits. This is clearly a disequilibrium situation. The first industry would be earning a lower than normal rate of profit while the second would earn a higher than normal rate.

In between these two cases there must be a third industry which has labor and means of production combined in the same proportions as the average. In this industry revenue freed by the fall of w would be exactly sufficient to pay the increased r. Therefore, there is no need for the price of this industry's product to change with changes in the distribution of the surplus between wages and profits.

Thus, changes in the distribution of income between wages and profits will in general necessitate changes in the relative price structure. In the case immediately above, the

62

balance can be restored by an increase in the price of the output of the first industry relative to the value of its means of production, and a fall in the price of the second relative to its means of production. For the deficit industry this price rise releases part of the revenues which previously purchased means of production to pav profits, and allows a given quantity of product to cover more of the total profit payment.

Here a major complication is introduced. It is not necessarily true that a fall in wages will cause a rise in the price of commodities produced by a deficit industry relative to its means of production. If these means of production were themselves produced with an even lower proportion of labor to means of production, the commodity could fall in value relative to its means of production if the fall in wages causes a greater increase in the value of the means of production than in the commodity itself. Sraffa concludes:

> These considerations dominate not only the price-relation of a product to its means of production but equally its relations to any other product.... The result is that the relative price of two products may move, with the fall of wages, in the opposite direction to what we might have expected on the basis of their respective 'proportions'.[8]

This is Ricardo's curious effect which lead to his despair on the standard of value. It is to Sraffa's credit that he has solved this classical problem of a standard of value independent of prices and distribution. Consider a commodity which is produced by the proportion of labor to means of production which exactly generates the revenue required by a higher rate of profit from a fall in wages. Call this the 'critical' proportion of labor to means of production. If the means of production entering into the production of this commodity were also produced by this 'critical' proportion and so on throughout the layers of production, then this commodity would not undergo a change in relative price as the wage/profit relation changed.

In order to find this 'critical' or 'balancing' ratio, recurrence in all lines of production is sufficient. Since we have introduced the wage as a share in surplus, the only ratio which is capable of recurring is the value ratio of the value of net product to value of the means of production where r = 1. In this case $\underline{r}$, the general rate of profit, is also the value ratio of the value of net output to the value of the means of production. It recurs in all production processes because it is the general rate of profits. This ingenious method for finding the 'critical' ratio where the proportion of labor to means of production are the same for input and output involves substituting the ratio of net product to means of production for the labor/means of production ratio. This is made possible by the assumption that labor's share comes from net product.

This 'balancing' ratio is called the Maximum rate of profits since it is the rate of profits which corresponds to a zero wage. This ratio is denoted $\underline{R}$.

In order to construct a standard of value we need a commodity produced by the balanced proportion described above.

Since it is unlikely that such a commodity can be found,
Sraffa uses a composite commodity. This is a group of basic
commodities which enter their own means of production in the
same proportions in which they enter total output. This
composite is denoted the Standard commodity, and the set of
production equations which produce this commodity is the
Standard system. It will be convenient to consider one unit of
this standard commodity to be the net national income produced
in the standard system when the entire labor force is employed.

Since in the standard system each commodity enters the
means of production in the same proportions it enters output,
the ratio of net product to means of production is the same for
each single commodity and also for the system taken as a whole.
This ratio is the Standard ratio, and it is independent of
prices as the following example illustrates:

$\frac{3}{16}$ L + 90t iron + 120t coal + 60 qr wheat → 180t iron

$\frac{3}{16}$ L + 30t iron + 75t coal + 90qr wheat → 270t coal

$\frac{6}{16}$ L + 30t iron + 30t coal + 150qr wheat → 360qr wheat.

In this system the aggregate means of production and total
output are composed of the same proportions of iron, coal, and
wheat. The aggregate means of production are 150t iron, 225t
coal, and 300qr wheat. Output consists of 180t iron, 270t coal,
and 360qr wheat. The proportions are 1t iron: 1½t coal: 2qr
wheat. The ratio of net output to means of production is
given by:

$$\frac{30I + 45C + 60W}{150I + 225C + 300W} \, ,$$

65

which can be written as

$$\frac{(30I + 45C + 60W)}{5(30I + 45C + 60W)} = \frac{1}{5},$$

which is the ratio of net product to means of production, or
R since this is a standard system. It should now be clear that
inserting the prices for iron, coal, and wheat will not influence this ratio since the prices will have the same effect
on the numerator as the denominator.

If we now distribute the standard national income between
wages and profits we can establish a relation between these
distributive shares and the standard ratio which holds for the
standard system. If we remember R is the ratio of net product
to means of production in this system we have

$$R = \frac{S}{M},$$

Where S represents the value of surplus and M is the value of
the means of production. Since the total profits are paid as
a percentage of the means of production advanced, we have

$$r = \frac{\text{total profits}}{M}$$

or

$$rM = \text{total profits}$$

Since wages (w) is a fraction of surplus we have

$$wS = \text{total wages}.$$

Now since S = total wages + total profits we can write:

$$S = rM + wS.$$

66

Substituting this into the expression for R gives:

$$R = \frac{rM + wS}{M} \, ,$$

Simplifying and rearranging terms gives the relation we desire:

$$r = R(1 - w).$$

This is a linear relation between wages and profit for each level of R in the standard system.

We must now establish that this linear relation has validity in an actual system as well as in the imaginary standard system. If the decisive role of the standard commodity derives from its being made up of the commodities in the national income and the means of production, then its applicability is limited to the standard system only, since the actual system will not be composed in the correct proportions. However, the standard commodity can serve the function of a standard of wages and profit even though the actual system is not in the correct proportions. In the standard system payment of wages leaves an amount of standard commodity to pay profits. Since profits are paid as standard commodity, the rate of profits in the standard system will be a homogeneous ratio of net product to means of production. It would appear there is no reason to believe that in the actual system payment of the equivalent of the same quantity of standard commodity for wages will leave a profit payment such that the value of this payment is in the same relation to the value of the means of production as the corresponding quantities in the standard

67

system. But, since the actual system and standard system are composed of the same production equations, only in different proportions, setting the wage in one also sets it in the other.

> The straight-line relation between the wage and the rate of profits will therefore hold in all cases, provided only that the wage is expressed in terms of the Standard product. The same rate of profits which in the Standard system is obtained as a ratio between quantities of commodities, will in the actual system result from the ratio of aggregate values.[9]

Sraffa then goes on to show how the equations which will give a set of multipliers which when applied to an actual system will appropriately change the proportions of output products and means of production such that a standard system results. Then he gives the equation for the standard national income which is the standard of value which is invariant to changes in prices and distribution. After a proof of the uniqueness of these multipliers, Sraffa makes use of the standard in a chapter on labor dating.

This chapter is of particular interest because it contains a demonstration of the impossibility of determining a quantity of capital independent of prices and distribution. The demonstration rests on showing, with an example, that if two commodities are produced by different time patterns of labor inputs, then the effects of compounding the rate of profits for each year before revenue is realized will cause reversals in the relative prices of the two commodities.

Sraffa proceeds in subsequent chapters to extend the basic analysis to joint product industries, fixed capital, rent, and

68

switches in the methods of production. While there is
considerable importance in this material especially since the
last chapter on switches of technique has produced a very
important debate in recent years, for our purposes we only need
a firm grasp of the essential model laid out above. This
provides the basics of Sraffa's type of value analysis wherein
value is seen as bounded by technical production requirements
and the necessity of paying a uniform rate of profits in all
industries.

Commentators on Sraffa have proceeded along three major
lines of argument.[10] The more conventional reviewers such as
Reder and Harrod have been disturbed by the lack of demand
equations in the determination of relative values.[11] More
sympathetic statements have come from Dobb, Meek, Robinson,
and Eatwell.[12] While Meek and Eatwell have been mainly
concerned with showing the basic similarity between Sraffa and
the earlier classical writers (particularly Ricardo and Marx),
Dobb and Robinson have focused primary attention on the
critique of the neoclassical theory of value and distribution.[13]

Meek argues that the main line of similarity between
Ricardo and Marx, on the one hand, and Sraffa, on the other,
lies in the problems in analysis introduced by the compounding
of profits throughout the period of production. This can be
attributed to the impinging upon simple commodity production,
in the Marxian sense, of capitalist production relations which
necessitates the payment of profits.[14] This means the rate of

profits now is greater than zero and the crude labor theory of
value is no longer applicable. This realization lead Ricardo
to search for an invariant standard of value, Marx to the theory
of production price, and Sraffa to the standard commodity.
Eatwell has shown the basic similarity between these puzzles
created by the labor theory of value. He has demonstrated
Sraffa's standard commodity is Marx's average commodity whose
price-to-value-of-labor relation is invariant to changes in the
rate of profit.[15] Sraffa's relation between wages, profit,
and R is, according to Eatwell, the answer to the Marxian
transformation problem which seeks to establish a functional
relation between surplus value and profits.

Sraffa's Production of Commodities by Means of
Commodities is devoted to the demonstration that not only
does such a composite commodity always exist, but also
that the relationship between the wage rate and the rate
of profit in terms of the physical division of the
composite commodity, a simple proportionate relation, is
exactly the same as that obtained for the economy as a
whole when the composite commodity, which Sraffa calls
the standard commodity, is used as the standard of value,
and hence the wage is expressed in units of this standard.
There is also an equally simple relationship between the
rate of surplus value, expressed as a ratio of surplus
labour time to necessary labour time in the production of
the standard commodity, and the rate of profit. In other
words, as in all cases of a commodity which is the only
input to its own production, there is a direct relationship betwen the rate of surplus value and the rate of
profit in the 'production' of the standard commodity.
When the standard commodity is used as 'money' of the
general system, the relation between the wage rate and
the profit rate is the same as if it were analyzed solely
in terms of the 'average'--the standard commodity.

Sraffa's standard commodity therefore possesses all
the characteristics which Marx sought in the 'average
commodity' which was to be the key to his solution of the
transformation problem.[16]

Since the third line of inquiry, typified by Robinson and
Dobb, is concerned with the critique of economic theory raised
by the propositions in Sraffa's book and since this critique,
though important, is tangential to our main line of argument,
we need not look in detail at what they have said, except to
note they have brought out Sraffa's analysis is clearly
opposed to the supply and demand analysis of conventional
theory. Robinson has observed

> when we are provided with a set of technical equations for
> production and a real wage rate which is uniform through-
> out the economy, there is no room for demand equations
> in the determination of equilibrium prices . . . in a
> market economy, either there may be a tendency towards
> uniformity of wages and the rate of profit in different
> lines of production, or prices may be governed by supply
> and demand, but not both.[17]

This line of inquiry will be developed more fully in the next
chapter.

We have now at our command an historical overview of the
development of the classical theory of value from Adam Smith
to Piero Sraffa. We have seen that it has been dominated by
the problems of analysis posed by the differing compositions
of capital, and how the effort to solve this problem has
ultimately lead to the development of a general equilibrium
model al a Dmitriev and Sraffa which determines prices and
profits simultaneously. However, in doing so many of the
features of the labor theory of value, such as its role in
determining relative prices and its role in analyzing the
essence of value, have been pushed into the background. The

next chapter will attempt to distill the fundamental features of the classical type of value analysis, and we shall attempt to show that the earlier labor theory and the modern commodities theory are within the same world view, and that, therefore, the differences between the two can be attributed to scientific refinement rather than to changes in vision.

NOTES

1. Piero Sraffa, Production of Commodities by Means of Commodities, (Cambridge: Cambridge University Press, 1960).

2. Ronald Meek, "Mr. Sraffa's Rehabilitation of Classical Economics," in Economics and Ideology and Other Essays, (London: Chapman and Hall, Ltd., 1967).

3. Sraffa, Production of Commodities, p. 3.

4. Ibid., p. 9.

5. Ibid., p. 9.

6. Ibid., p. 9.

7. Ibid., p. 11.

8. Ibid., p. 13.

9. Ibid., p. 23.

10. We could perhaps say four here because there have been several Marxists who have attempted to show that Sraffa's analysis is a departure from rather than a contribution to the Marxian value theory. See, for example, Michael Lebowitz, "The Crisis of Economic Theory," Science and Society 37 (1973-74): 385-403, Bob Rowthorn, "Neo-Classicism, Neo-Ricardianism, and Marxism," New Left Review 86 (1974): 63-87, and Frank Roosevelt, "Controversies in Economic Theory Cambridge Economics as Commodity Fetishism, Review of Radical Political Economics 7(4, 1975): 1-32.

11. Roy F. Harrod, "Review of Sraffa," Economic Journal 71 (284, 1961): 783-787. M.W. Reder, "Review," American Economic Review 51 (4, 1961): 688-695.

12. Maurice Dobb, "The Sraffa System and Critique of the Neo-Classical Theory of Distribution," in A Critique of Economic Theory, edited by Hunt and Schwartz (Harmondsworth, Middlesex, England: Penguin Books, Ltd., 1972), pp. 281-303. Joan Robinson, "Prelude to a Critique of Economic Theory," in Hunt and Schwartz, pp. 197-204. Meek, "Mr. Sraffa's Rehabilitation of Classical Economics," John Eatwell, "Controversies in the Theory of Surplus Value: Old and New," Science and Society 38 (3, 1974): 281-303, and Eatwell, "Mr. Sraffa's Standard Commodity and the Rate of Exploitation," Quarterly Journal of Economics 89 (375, 1975): 543-555.

13. This refers to the reswitching debate ignited by Sraffa's

discussion of switches in methods of production.

14. Meek, "Mr. Sraffa's Rehabilitation of Classical Economics," p. 168.

15. Eatwell, "Controversies in the Theory of Surplus Values," pp. 300-302.

16. Ibid., pp. 301-302.

17. Robinson, "Prelude to a Critique of Economic Theory," p. 202. Cf. Dobb, Theories of Value and Distribution, p. 257.

4. The Essence of the Classical Tradition

We come now to the problem of looking at the classical tradition as a whole. Is it possible to group together Smith, Ricardo, Marx, and Sraffa in a common school of thought? Several ideas have been put forward in other attempts to look at the similarity between these writers. For example, Sraffa himself has declared his work reminiscent of the older classics because

> the investigation is concerned exclusively with such properties of an economic system as do not depend on changes in the scale of production or in the proportions of 'factors'[1]

Ricardo also insisted that his theory of value and distribution is based on this same idea:

> It appears to me that one great cause of our difference in opinion . . . is that you have always in your mind the immediate and temporary effects of particular changes-- whereas I put these immediate and temporary effects quite aside, and fix my whole attention on the permanent state of things which will result from them.[2]

Furthermore, Dobb has pointed to the idea of wages as an independent datum as evidence of the similarity between Sraffa and the early classics,[3] while Meek has pointed out the "logical historical"[4] method which runs throughout from Smith to Sraffa.[5] The labor theory of value is applicable to the case where

profit is zero. This is a logical starting point for a simplified analysis as well as a model of a pre-capitalist exchange
society. The historical appearance of a separate class of
capitalists gaining profits alters the theory of value. Profits
now vary and are greater than zero. As we have seen above,
incorporation of a positive rate of profit into a determinate
theory of value has been a dominate theme among these writers.
Furthermore, Eatwell has convincingly demonstrated continuity
in the answers advanced by showing the basic similarity between
Ricardo's corn, Marx's industry of average composition, and
Sraffa's standard commodity.[6] All three are based on the idea
of a commodity which is its own means of production and the
means of those means, etc., such that production conditions of
this commodity govern the aggregate rate of profits since this
is the only commodity for which the value ratio of net revenue
to value of means of production depends solely on the physical
ratio of surplus product to necessary product. Perhaps more
basic is Dobb's observation that the Sraffa system is a

> rehabilitation of the Ricardo-Marx approach to the problems
> of value and distribution from the side of production;
> with the consequent result that relative prices are
> independent of the pattern of consumption and demand.[7]

THE CLASSICAL VISION: SUPPLY AND DEMAND

We can now begin to piece together the underlying vision
which gives rise to the distinctly classical type of value
theory. Perhaps the most obvious starting point is with Dobb's
point that classical analysis focuses on production, ignoring

76

the phenomenon of consumer demand. This is a basic feature of
all classical analysis, and, indeed, is the one most frequently
criticized by the neoclassical school. We will examine the
classical value theory to discover if this is a legitimate
result of the logic of the system or merely the result of
assuming the special case of constant returns to scale. This
will lead us further behind the scenes to the classical view of
the economic problem as production considered both as the physical problem of maintaining and expanding the productive system
by producing a subsistence and a surplus product,[8] and as the
social problem of shaping viable institutions over the secular
long run. We shall see that classical theory proceeds on the
physical and the social rather than the subjective and individ-
ualistic level of analysis.[9] This points us to the dominance of
production as a physical and social process as the crux of the
classical vision; physical because resources and concrete human
labor are expended (not "productive services" as more modern
writers suggest[10]); social because the productive process is
viewed as being undertaken in a definite social environment
which is characterized by a social division of labor making
for a high degree of interdependence among people and a class
division between workers, landlords, and capitalists. Bringing
these points together, we shall argue the classical approach to
value theory can be labeled the "materialist conception of
economic life" which means a classical economist sees the
economic process as an interaction between the forces of

production, i.e. the physical aspects of the production process, and the relations of production, i.e. the social aspects of the production process.

Further, although this conception emerges with Adam Smith, it develops greater clarity with the successive contributions of Ricardo and Marx, and, from a technical point of view, Sraffa. There is an "extended present"[11] of classical theory which allows it to be looked at as a whole. Chronologically more recent work can illuminate implicit relationships in older work and vice versa.

We begin with the non-price-determining role of demand. Ricardo frequently insisted that in his view supply and demand had very little to do with price formation:

> You say demand and supply regulates value--this I think is saying nothing, . . . --it is supply which regulates value--and supply is itself controlled by comparative cost of production.[12]

Similarly, Marx noted, "the exchange of commodities is evidently an act characterized by a total abstraction from use-value."[13] This in no way implies that demand is totally ignored in classical value analysis. On the contrary, Meek has pointed out several ways in which demand is important; it is a prerequisite for exchange value, a determinate of the proportion of the labor force allocated to each sector of the economy, and a determinate of monopoly prices. Changes in demand will also cause changes in the market price of a commodity.[14]

Turning now to twentieth century classicism, namely

78

Sraffa's model of price determination, we can give a much more specific analysis of the passive role which consumer demand plays in the classical framework. In commenting upon Sraffa's system Joan Robinson has observed that

> supply and demand has nothing to bite on. The composition of output may be influenced by the distribution of net income between workers and capitalists (for instance, more investment goods when the share of profits is high) but prices, in given technical conditions, are determined solely by the rate of profit.[15]

We can certainly see from Sraffa's equations that prices are indeed determinate, given the level of the real wage if labor shares in the surplus, without demand equations. Hence, mathematically demand is superfluous. However, we can gain more economic meaning if we compare Sraffa's price determining system of equations with a neoclassical system of price determination. First, let us recall Sraffa's system. The general equilibrium is given by K price equations:

$$(A_a P_a + B_a P_b + \ldots + K_a P_k)(k + r) + L_a w = AP_a$$
$$(A_b P_a + B_b P_b + \ldots + K_b P_k)(1 + r) + L_b w = BP_b$$
$$\cdot \cdot \cdot \cdot \cdot \cdot \cdot \cdot \cdot \cdot \cdot \cdot \cdot \cdot \cdot \cdot \cdot \cdot \cdot \cdot \cdot \cdot$$
$$(A_k P_a + B_k P_b + \ldots + K_k P_k)(1 + r) + L_k w = KP_k,$$

and a price equation for the numeraire commodity which is the net income considered as a composite commodity:

$$[A - (A_a + A_b + \ldots + A_k)]P_a + [B - (B_a + B_b + \ldots + B_k)]P_b + \ldots + [K - (K_a + K_b + \ldots + K_k)]P_k = 1.$$

All elements in the last equation are considered non-negative since the system is in a self-replacing state ex-hypothesi.

This gives K + 1 equations to determine K prices, $\underline{r}$, and $\underline{w}$.

Once $\underline{w}$ is exogenously specified, the system becomes determinate.

By way of contrast consider the following neoclassical model.[16]

Let

a_{ij} = the quantity of factor j needed to produce a unit of good i
q_j = price of factor j
R_j = quantity of factor j available
S_i = supply of good i
D_i = demand for good i

If there are n goods and r factors, then price equations for the goods are given by:

$$a_{11}q_1 + a_{12}q_2 + \ldots + a_{1r}q_r = P_1$$
$$a_{21}q_1 + a_{22}q_2 + \ldots + a_{2r}q_r = P_2$$
$$\cdot \quad \cdot \quad \cdot \quad \cdot \quad \cdot \quad \cdot \quad \cdot \quad \cdot \quad \cdot \quad \cdot \quad \cdot \quad \cdot \quad \cdot \quad \cdot \quad \cdot \quad \cdot$$
$$a_{n1}q_1 + a_{n2}q_2 + \ldots + a_{nr}q_r = P_n.$$

This gives n equations, but since both q's and p's are unknowns, there are n + r unknown quantities, an indeterminate situation. The neoclassical theory rectifies this by introducing demand equations.

$$D_1 = F_1 (P_1, \ldots, P_n)$$
$$D_2 = F_2 (P_1, \ldots, P_n)$$
$$\cdot \quad \cdot \quad \cdot \quad \cdot \quad \cdot \quad \cdot \quad \cdot \quad \cdot \quad \cdot \quad \cdot \quad \cdot \quad \cdot$$
$$D_n = F_n (P_1, \ldots, P_n).$$

However, the system is still not determinate since we have introduced quantity demanded as a new variable. The system is closed by introducing the equilibrium conditions:

$$S_1 = D_1, \; S_2 = D_2, \; \ldots, \; S_n = D_n$$

for all goods, and

$$R_1 = a_{11}S_1 + a_{21}S_2 + \ldots + a_{n1}S_n$$
$$R_2 = a_{12}S_1 + a_{22}S_2 + \ldots + a_{n2}S_n$$
$$\cdots \cdots \cdots \cdots \cdots \cdots \cdots \cdots$$
$$R_r = a_{1r}S_1 + a_{2r}S_2 + \ldots + a_{nr}S_n$$

for all factors.

Since R_j's and a_{ij}'s are assumed to be known quantities, the last set of equations adds no new variables. We, therefore, have $2n + r$ unknowns: $D_i \; (= S_i)$, P_i, and q_i, and $2n + r$ equations: n price equations, n demand equations, and r factor utilization equations.

Aside from the fact that in Sraffa's model quantities are given exogenously, while in the neoclassical model they are variable, the most important reason why demand is necessary in the latter but not in the former is that the neoclassical model makes a distinction between goods and factors while the Sraffa model does not. For Sraffa there are only commodities appearing as both input and output, while the neoclassical model pictures productive services as being combined to produce a distinctly different product. Instead of wheat, coal, and iron combining to produce wheat, coal, and iron we have services of land owners, capital owners, and laborers combining to produce wheat, coal, and iron. Hence, since the neoclassical school places such a strong emphasis on individuals' subjective feelings, the interface between consumption and

81

factor supply is conceived as of primary importance in the pricing process, and the circular flow of goods from sector to sector is thus broken.

By contrast, for the classical school this interface is essentially unimportant. Is there a legitimate reason for this position? It is our contention there is. If we remember that Sraffa's equations depict the basic sector of an economy, and if we realize this is a generalized form of the classical notion of subsistence, i.e. that portion of production which goes to maintain the system, then we can see two things. First, this fund of commodities goes for workers'consumption and means of production replacement and the workers portion is the demand placed on the system by consumers (workers).[17] Second, at any given stage of historical development it is reasonable to assume this demand is a fixed quantity in the aggregate,[18] since it represents consumption essential to the maintenance of the system, i.e. workers consumption plus means of production replacement. A system of social production existing in historical time must be assumed to be in a self-replacing state. As such, if the price of basics expressed interms of the standard commodity rose relative to non-basics because of diminishing returns, then consumption out of surplus, not out of this maintenance fund, would be sacrificed. None of the physical relations in the basic sector would change, hence none of the prices relative to each other would alter. Only the portion of surplus in total output would fall. This

82

reflects the logical role of consumption in a model of
reproduction. Consumption is part of the maintenance of the
system of reproduction rather than an end of the economic
process. Thus, the theory of demand is replaced by the
historically given production coefficients.

Economists generally view the role of demand as predicated
upon the existence of either increasing or decreasing returns
to scale. There remains consideration of the general relation
of quantity supplied to cost. Even though the production
coefficients are specified will not a small change in quantity
alter them because of increasing or decreasing returns to
scale?

Since it is important to note at this point the contexts
within which returns to scale are relevant, a short digression
on the historical development of Sraffa's thought is in order.
In his path breaking 1926 article, "The Laws of Returns Under
Competitive Conditions," Sraffa critiques the Marshallian
supply curve analysis in a way which foreshadows his position
in Production of Commodities.[19] The laws of increasing and
decreasing returns are of such a nature as to be either
severely limited in scope or to violate the independence of
supply and demand. In the case of diminishing returns if an
industry uses a small amount of a non-reproducable factor,
such as land, an increase in the industry's scale will not
cause an increase in the price of the factor. There will be
a flat long run supply curve. If the industry in question uses

83

a large quantity, increasing its scale will cause the factor
price to rise. However, this will affect all industries using
the factor, and since it is likely these other industries
produce substitute commodities, it is very possible there will
be a change in demand for the product of the industry in question. The independence of supply and demand is violated.
Therefore,

> the imposing structure of diminishing returns is avail-
> able only for the study of that minute class of commodi-
> ties in the production of which the whole of a factor
> of production is employed.[20]

The case is similar for the law of increasing returns.
Large scale production may result in declining supply price
for an industry because of either economies external or
internal to the firm. If they are internal they will violate
the assumption of competition. If they are external they must
still be internal to the industry otherwise the **independence** of
supply and demand are again violated. The applicability of
the law is again reduced to a small number of cases.

> Those economies which are external from the point of view
> of the firm, but internal as regards the industry in its
> aggregate, constitute precisely the class which is
> seldom met with.[21]

The old classical tradition of basing competitive price on
cost factors alone seems to be the best available.

At this point Sraffa saw two possible avenues of development. Either maintain the concept of free competition and
develop a general equilibrium with diminishing returns to a
constant factor or abandon competition. In 1926 he took the

84

latter path and the theory of monopolistic competition followed. <u>Production of Commodities</u> takes the first path. We
do not know exactly why he abandoned the path originally
sketched out. However, we do know he was moving in a direction of completely discarding the Marshallian price theory[22]
and that imperfect competition proved a failure as an alternative general theory of price.[23]

It is our contention he took up the general equilibrium
approach precisely to construct a superior general theory of
value. In taking up this approach he realized the whole question of returns to scale is completely irrelevant under static
conditions of economic reproduction.[24] Thus, he states in the
preface of <u>Production of Commodities</u>:

> Anyone accustomed to think in terms of the equilibrium of
> demand and supply may be inclined, on reading these pages,
> to suppose that the argument rests on a tacit assumption
> of constant returns in all industries.... In fact...no
> such assumption is made.[25]

The essential nature of the general system of reproduction is
such that one process cannot expand without expanding the whole,
since inputs are produced within the system. Therefore, the
relation of prices, wages, and profits to quantity of output is
a matter of analyzing the process of growth. It has no part to
play in the static model of simple reproduction. The quantity
of output is specified with reference to the whole, and is
determined by the size of the available labor force in conjunction with the prevailing technique and the condition of full
employment. The issue of diminishing returns arising from

constant or non-reproducable factors is a dynamic phenomenon which enters when considering the path of expansion. Conceptually this might be handled by focusing on R, the aggregate rate of surplus. If the expanding system encounters diminishing returns R would tend to fall as the value of basics rises relative to non-basics.

Some might argue the approach which emphasizes the system of reproduction is reasonably valid for an economy, such as England's in the time of Smith and Ricardo, which is dominated the subsistence, or reproductive sector, but is not valid for a modern capitalist economy in which production and consumption of surplus is much more dominant. However, this is not the main reason why classical analysis places such strong emphasis on the maintenance sector. Focusing on maintenance, we have isolated a sector whose output is a composite commodity which enters as means of production into the production processes of all commodities including itself. Because of its very nature, Ricardo and Marx conclude that production conditions in this sector determine the aggregate rate of profits, since profit in this sector is a value ratio which is determined by a purely physical ratio. Hence, prices of other industries must adjust to achieve equality of profit rates.[26] Similarly, in Sraffa the basic sector, which is equivalent to the classical subsistence sector, determines R, the maximum rate of profits. The importance of this sector is derived from its role in the determination of prices and profits which reflect physical

production requirements and which therefore determine boundaries within which non-basic prices may move. Violation of
these boundaries will cause changes in R, possibly sacrificing
the viability of the whole system.

THE CLASSICAL VISION: PRODUCTION

We can now see the importance of the division of the
economy into a subsistence sector and a surplus sector in the
classical view on the relative unimportance of demand. This
follows as a logical corollary of isolating the basic sector
and treating it in a static general equilibrium model. The
basic sector is isolated for study because it determines the
aggregate or maximum rate of profits. This dominance of a
distinction between subsistence and surplus is also a reflec-
tion of the classical conception of the economic problem.

> What then is the economic problem suggested by the labour
> theory? In its simplest form, the labour theory depicts
> a primitive agricultural community, self-sufficient, and
> having only a rudimentary system of exchange. In this
> setting it is natural to look upon production as the
> struggle of man against nature and to measure wealth in
> terms of the physical product of labour.[27]

Therefore, growth is a central goal, and surplus as the fund
available to create and maintain a larger capital stock and
supply of labor becomes a central feature of the classical
analysis. However, more fundamentally, the direct result of
this approach is a physical, objective, value analysis rather
than a subjective one. Production is viewed as a physical
process, and relative exchange values are determined by the

physical proportions of commodities which are dictated by the
historically given methods of production.[28] This is most
clearly seen in Sraffa's model of wheat and iron production,
as well as in Marx's aggregate model of circulation. The
exchange ratio of 1t iron for 10qr wheat is determined by the
needs of each sector for replacement. This idea of the overriding importance of physical proportions has been an important aspect of the classical theory since before Smith.[29]

Moreover, determination of the aggregate rate of profits
proceeds on the physical level. From Ricardo's corn model to
Marx's theory of surplus value to Sraffa's standard commodity,
the theory of profit is approached by showing how a physical
ratio can be derived which is reflected in and equal to the
value ratio which appears as the rate of profits, or, in
Sraffa, the maximum rate of profits.

Meek has so well summarized this whole idea of the
economic problem and what it means for the classical economic
categories that we feel no embarrassment in quoting his
explanation at length:

> In a predominantly agricultural economy there may well be
> a tendency for both labour and land to be conceived as
> equally 'active' factors in the productive process--labour
> because it appears to be the indispensable initiator of
> that process and land because of the 'activity' displayed
> by the regenerative powers of the soil. But in an indus-
> trial economy, where by the aid of 'ingenious labour' man
> is able to produce an abundance of material wealth
> undreamed of in former times, nature begins to be
> conceived, not as an active co-partner in the business of
> getting a living, but as little more than a passive sleep-
> ing partner. In manufacture it is immediately obvious
> that man is the dominant partner, but in agriculture

88

> nature does not yield her former authority without a
> struggle. The continued existence of rent seems to prove
> that nature still 'labours along with man' in the fields
> and pastures. But, when it is demonstrated that the
> existence of rent is due not to nature's beneficence but
> to her niggardliness, that such assistance as she does
> give is given in all occupations, and not in agriculture
> alone, and that in any event it is given freely, without
> any cost to man--then the expenditure of human labour is
> revealed as the only fundamental form of cost or sacrifice
> common to all branches of production. Human labour begins
> to appear as the basic universal and active cost element,
> always to be found in operation when productive activity
> results in a value difference between input and output....
> The expenditure of human labour power remained the basic
> social cost. The value of the gross national product
> then, could be measured by the quantity of living and
> dead labour embodied in it. To replace this expended
> labour cost society the amount of labour which it was
> necessary to devote to the production of subsistence goods
> for the labourers. The difference between these two
> quantities of labour measured the net social gain--the
> surplus or net revenue resulting from productive activ-
> ity.[30]

Thus, the classical view of the economic problem as humanity's

struggle to produce leads us to the explanation for the phys-

ical, objective, rather than the subjective, psychological

mode of analysis. This in turn illuminates the concern with

growth, the distinction between surplus and subsistence, and

the style of national income accounting. In addition, we gain

valuable insight into the nature of classical value theory as

depending on physical proportions, and we gain insight into the

choice of labour as the sole creator of value.

THE CLASSICAL VISION: THE SOCIAL FRAMEWORK

Thus far we have looked at production as a purely physical

process, and we have gained important knowledge about several

aspects of the classical approach. To proceed further in our analysis we must now realize that in this approach production is both a physical process of people working with **nature** and a social process of people cooperating with each other within a definite type of social organization. Indeed, as Meek has pointed out, it was the recognition of the specifically capitalist mode of production characterized by the existence of a capitalist class receiving a uniform rate of profit on their investment which was one of the seminal contributions of Adam Smith which lead to the development of the classical school.[31, 32]

It is the emergence of a highly developed social division of labor with its high level of human interdependence which is the historical event which gives rise to exchange value as a phenomenon of human interaction of such prime importance as to occupy the thought processes of the intellectual community. This in turn produces a new field of inquiry called political economy. Therefore, in the classical view value arises in a particular social system which depends on exchange for its continued existence. Since this web of interdependence is based upon the social division of labor, it is not surprising that the classical economists look upon exchange, which is the link between people, as exchange of different concrete types of social labor. It is but a small leap from this realization to a theory which attempts to draw a quantitative relation between labor and exchange value.[33] A good acquires value

> by virtue of the fact that it is the product of the labour
> of an individual or group of individuals in a society
> which is characterized by and dependent upon the mutual
> interchange of the products of the separate labours of
> individuals. The exchange of commodities is in essence
> the exchange of social activities. The value relation-
> ship between commodities which manifests itself in the
> act of exchange is in essence the reflection of a
> relationship between men as producers.[34]

Value is a social relation, it serves to unify and coordinate

the social activity of production which is carried on by

individual producers. It is the mediator between the indivi-

dual and the society of which he or she is a part.

It is interesting to note that just as Sraffa helps us

understand the general equilibrium aspects of the classical

theory which are implicit in Ricardo, so also Marx's value

analysis helps us in a similar way. Although Smith and

Ricardo never used terms such as "social relation" it should be

clear that by focusing on production and the division of labor

these ideas are contained in their constructions.[35]

Perhaps we can gain further insight by looking again at

Sraffa's wheat and iron model. As stated above the value

ratio of 1 to 10 is determined by the technical requirements

of production. However, to then say that value is a purely

technical relation would be absurd, even in the highly

abstract logic of Sraffa. It is the social nature of produc-

tion which causes a technical relation to appear as a value

relation. Therefore, a complete understanding of thi-

would realize the dependence of classical va

dual relation of people to nature (productio

people (social interdependence). To use Marxian terminology, value is an historical category specific to commodity society. This institutional specification is the starting point of classical theory.

This identification of the specific and temporal social environment characteristic of a market society is only one of the two ways of explaining how value relations occur. Capitalist society is a particular form of commodity society which has evolved historically from simple commodity production, and which became the object of inquiry for classical economists. In particular this historical form is characterized by a new class of property owner, capitalist, gaining a new type of income, profit, which somehow did not derive from buying cheap and selling dear, but rather was gained by employing wage labor whose productivity was such as to return a surplus to the employer. Hence, the relationship within the production process between laborer and capitalist gradually appeared as a crucial problem in the theory of value, and, in Marx, as the key to the whole process of capitalist development. Classical theory tends to proceed in a "logical-historical" fashion beginning with a hypothetical simple commodity production, and then analyzing the changes brought about by the emergence of capitalist production. This appears particularly vivid in Smith's distinction between the "early and rude state" where labor time determined value and the advanced state of society where labor shared the produce with landlords and capitalists.

92

It is also true of Ricardo's and Sraffa's situations of zero profit, and of course it is true of Marx's distinction between simple and capitalist commodity production.

Thus, the theroy of value is altered to take into account historical, institutional data. Labor values are replaced by prices of production. Value becomes a function of distribution as well as physical requirements and social interdependence. However, the influence of distribution is itself a conjunction between the physical and social worlds. The physical situation indicates the existence of a surplus above mere survival. The social arrangement of the production process provides that the surplus accrues as property income divided between landlord and capitalist before the market transactions occur. Thus, we have a second determinant of value. Classical theory must be understood as having for its characteristic problematic a threefold relationship between the technical, physical world, the social interdependence brought about by the division of labor, and the relationships within production between laborers and capitalists.[36] All of these processes occur behind the veil of money which is established in the market where commodities are exchanged and where their value appears as a relation of things to money. These processes are considered prior to market relations because they are conceived of as regulating market relations in the secular long run. Therefore,

> The classical labour theory is the embodiment of their
> belief that market phenomena could only be fully under-
> stood by penetrating below the surface to the social
> relations among men as producers which ultimately deter-
> mined their market relations.[37]

We have in the classical tradition a vision which might best be

labeled the "materialist conception of economic society" which

is analogous to Marx's conception of history. Just as Marx

viewed history as a progression of modes of production, each

characterized by different forms of the forces of production

and the social relations of production, and each developing

and changing constantly in response to the complex interactions

between these forces and relations and within the relations

themselves, classical theory rests on a similar conception

applied to economic categories.[38] If we realize that what we

have been calling the physical world is precisely Marx's

forces of production and the social relations we have elab-

orated are his relations of production, it becomes immediately

clear that this threefold inter-relation referred to above

is none other than the application of Marx's basic conception

to the theory of value. Seen from this broad perspective as

a specific instance of the sweep of human development called

history it is not surprising to find demand pushed to the

background, since in this view demand is taken as historically

determined by the specific form of the relations of production

which are ultimately important in determining the distribution

of income and social class.[39]

We have now come full circle. By starting out with the "glaring" lack of demand analysis in classical theory, we have penetrated to the classical vision of production as a physical-social process which determines exchange relations as the center piece of the classical tradition. In this view demand is not ignored, but rather approached via production as a quantity determined by the maintenance requirements of the system. Moreover, in the broad sweep of development, which is the forte of classical analysis, demand is a purely passive responder to changes in the methods of production, and to changes in the labor-capital relation. To sum up, in the classical view value is a social relation which reflects and is bounded by underlying technical interdependence because of the specific historically determined type of social environment in which production takes place.

NOTES

1. Sraffa, Production of Commodities, p. v. It should also be noted Sraffa points out that this stance makes his model non-marginal.

2. Ricardo to Malthus, Jan. 24, 1818, Works and Correspondence, Vol. 7, p. 120.

3. Dobb, Theories of Value and Distribution, p. 261.

4. Ronald Meek, "Karl Marx's Economic Method," in Studies in the Labour Theory of Value, pp. 302-303.

5. Meek, Studies in the Labour Theory of Value, p. xlii.

6. Eatwell, "Controversies in the Theory of Surplus Value."

7. Dobb, Theories of Value and Distribution, p. 252.

8. Dobb, Political Economy and Capitalism, p. 19.

9. Hla Myint, Theories of Welfare Economics, (Cambridge, Massachusetts: Harvard University Press, 1948). The notion of classical theory proceeding on the physical level and neoclassical on the subjective level is a dominate theme of this book.

10. Knight, "The Ricardian Theory of Production and Distribution," pp. 4-5.

11. Kenneth F. Boulding, "After Samuelson, Who Needs Adam Smith," History of Political Economy 3(2, 1971): 225-237.

12. Ricardo to Malthus, October 9, 1820, Works and Correspondence, Vol. 8, p. 279.

13. Marx, Capital, Vol. 1, p. 45.

14. Meek, Studies in the Labour Theory of Value, p. 178.

15. Joan Robinson, "Piero Sraffa and the Rate of Exploitation," New Left Review 31(1965): 31.

16. The model is taken from Gustav Cassel, "The Mechanism of Pricing," in Price Theory, edited by Harry Townsend, Harmondsworth, Middlesex, England: Penguin Books, Ltd., 1973), pp. 93-119.

17. Cf. "consumer demand may be said to be reflected in the relative magnitudes of the scalars of the equations of production." (A. L. Levine, "This Age of Leontief . . . and Who? An Interpretation," Journal of Economic Literature 12(3, 1974):879.

18. Consider the following passage on the relationship between the demand and supply theory and the marginal utility theory of value. "The demand and supply theory lays emphasis upon the entire volume of demand; it takes for granted variability of part of the demand. The marginal utility theory lays emphasis upon the variable part of demand; the existence of a large unvarying demand is taken for granted. (Department of Political Economy, University of Chicago, Outlines of Economics, Developed in a Series of Problems, (Chicago: University of Chicago Press, 1914), p. 50. Following a similar line of thought to look at classical and neoclassical analysis, it would appear there is room for a grand synthesis based upon the concept of a fixed part and a variable part of demand. The fixed part is relevant to the analysis of the classical subsistence sector which determines basic prices, profits, and the rate of growth. The variable part would apply to the analysis of the prices of non-basics which are determined by supply and demand.

19. Piero Sraffa, "The Laws of Returns Under Competitive Conditions," Economic Journal 36(1926): 535-550.

20. Ibid., p. 539.

21. Ibid., p. 540.

22. Dennis Robertson, G. F. Shove, and P. Sraffa,"Increasing Returns and the Representative Firm: A Symposium," Economic Journal 40(1930): 93.

23. James A. Clifton, "Competition and the Evolution of the Capitalist Mode of Production," Cambridge Journal of Economics 1(2, 1977): 142.

24. Ibid., p. 140.

25. Sraffa, Production of Commodities, p. v.

26. See Above, p. 28.

27. Myint, Theories of Welfare Economics, pp. 2-3. See also Dobb, Political Economy and Capitalism, p. 19: "The crux of the economic problem as this theory represented it, and as had been traditionally viewed, lay in the struggle of man with nature to wrest a livelihood for himself under various forms of production at various stages of history."

28. Perhaps this is an appropriate place to include a short note on the assumption of given methods of production, or fixed factor proportions in deference to modern terminology. This simply rests on the notion that, time being irreversible, production methods in existence can be taken as given. See also Schumpeter, History of Economic Analysis, p. 908.

29. The idea goes back at least as far as the Physiocrats in the Tablean Economique.

30. Ronald Meek, "The Decline of Ricardian Economics in England," pp. 53-54.

31. Ronald Meek, Studies in the Labour Theory of Value, p. 24ff.

32. Although we did not touch upon the idea of a uniform rate of profit above, since it is tied in with the social, institutional reference point of classical analysis, this recognition was an important reason why classical theory concentrates on production, ignoring demand: "It became more and more clear that under competitive conditions profit at a reasonably regular rate would be earned on capital . . . and that this profit must be regarded as originating in production rather than exchange." (Ibid., p. 27.)

This uniform rate of profit has been an important feature in all classical value theory, and it is a supporting pillar in the determination of relative prices from the side of production.

33. Meek, Studies in the Labour Theory of Value, p. 39.

34. Ibid., p. 62.

35. Althusser, Reading Capital, p. 170.

36. It should now be apparent that there is no departure from the basic vision when distribution between labor and capital, the wage-profit relation, is brought in as a second determinant of value. Value still arises in the conjunction between a physical and a social process, only now there are two social processes simultaneously at work. The price system of this latter, more complicated system, is intended to be closer to capitalist reality, however, it is important not to drop the value system of simple commodity production because only here does the dependence of value on the physical system come through so strikingly. Also it is necessary not to lose sight of the idea of profit determined as a value ratio: which equals a physical ratio.

37. Ronald Meek, "Marginalism and Marxism," in The Marginal Revolution in Economics, edited by R. D. Collison Black, et al, (Durham, North Carolina: Duke University Press, 1973), p. 234.

38. Meek, Studies in the Labour Theory of Value, p. 130.

39. Althusser, Reading Capital, pp. 166-167.

5. Perspectives on the History of Economic Thought and Beyond

We have reached the point in our inquiry where we wish to make statements of an interpretative nature about the history of economics as a whole, and then to look beyond historical development to a plan of future research wherein some ideas of how this understanding of the classical theory might be fruit-fully applied to questions of social policy. Since policy has historically been the goal of economic inquiry, this is the ultimate objective. Abstract theorizing receives its justifica-tion only if it intersects with the social scene of the times.

This historical discussion is divided into two parts. First, we will look at the classical tradition separately to elaborate Sraffa's improvements in the analysis. Implicitly we will be tackling the whole question of progress within this tradition. Second, we will look at the history of classical economics as a portion of the general history of economic thought. This leads to some important criticism of the lead-ing ideas of the historians of economic thought. Consequently we will attempt to develop the general outlines of a more complete and accurate account than has been advanced.

THE DEVELOPMENT OF ECONOMICS: SRAFFA AND THE CLASSICAL TRADITION

In assessing Sraffa's role in the development of classical economics we must be very careful what we mean by progress. Specifically, we do not mean that progress absolves one of the necessity of reading earlier works on the same subject on the grounds the latest treatise, being the most advanced, contains all of the insights but none of the errors of the past. Rather, we shall consider progress to be manifested by solutions to old problems,[1] clarification of previous confusion, and more accurate perception of interaction and interdependence in the economic system as a whole.[2] This view of progress leaves open the possibility that earlier writers have completed some aspects of the analysis which future writers need not repeat. Hence, only an historical investigation will gain a complete understanding. This is because the classical tradition has an "extended present". Ricardo, Marx, and Sraffa must be looked at as a whole each taking particular problems from his predecessor for further refinement, but also each not specifically addressing other areas of importance. For example, Sraffa does not address the question of exploitation and the meaning of the concept value. Nevertheless, his analysis is an important contribution to this tradition. Therefore, to argue that the Sraffa system is contrary to Marxian analysis on the grounds he does not explicitly deal with Marx's theory of exploitation and history is wrong.[3] Sraffa's analysis addresses a difficult

101

technical problem which is central to the analysis of prices of production in the classical system. This is the relation of distribution to value and the concomitant need for an invariant standard of value. Little would be gained if he started from the very beginning of classical value analysis, elaborating its relation to an historical mode of production, and then transforming labor values into prices of production. All of this had been done by predecessors. It is still, of course, possible Sraffa himself would want to deny an affinity toward Marxism, but his differences, if any, are not evident in his published work.

Considered in this light, Sraffa has made some definite contributions to the classical theory of value. From the point of view of solving technical problems he has solved the problem of an invariant standard of value, circumvented the transformation problem without departing from the classical vision, and taken a major step towards operationalizing the theory by replacing labor time with physical commodities used in actual production processes. First, it is clear the standard commodity solves Ricardo's problem of absolute value, since it is demonstrable that this commodity does in fact remain unaffected by changes in distribution. It serves as the system in which the rate of surplus for the actual system is determined. Reckoning wages in terms of standard commodity, a linear relation is deduced between wages and profits for a given rate of surplus. Second, by setting up a system of simultaneous equations, and by applying a uniform rate of profits to the value of the means of production in each industry, the system is determined for prices of production from the beginning. He also shows this is completely compatible with a labor embodied theory provided labor is dated and profit is earned on past labor for each year from its embodiment to realization in the final product. Either way, formally correct solutions for prices of production result without the need for transformations which seem to bear no relation to the real-world pricing process. This was also true of Dmitriev's analysis:

> both Dmitriev and Sraffa provide the correct solution to the determination of prices of production, of the kind sought by Marx, but their prices are not, as in Marx, a transformed form of labour values; they are determined directly from technology and the real wage rate, without the intermediate role of labour values.[4]

As for the transformation of surplus value into profit, which Baumol argues was the one Marx was really interested in,[5] Eatwell has argued Sraffa's linear equation relating wages and profits and surplus is the solution to this aspect of the transformation problem.[6] Third, by conducting the analysis in terms of quantities of physical goods rather than labor hours, Sraffa has made the system more operational. While concrete labor hours can be reduced to hours of abstract labor without reference to actual market determined wages, goods used in production processes can be more easily differentiated on the basis of physical properties which give them their usefulness. Moreover, since each good is defined by the goods entering its production, and since each good in turn enters all production processes including its own, values can be determined, once the wage or profit rate is set, without actually adding heterogeneous goods together, i.e. the ability to define goods does not hinge on knowing prices as does the ability to define a quantity of capital.

Consideration of the transformation problem and the notion of goods producing themselves leads us to another aspect of Sraffa's contribution, which is more powerful and noteworthy than those considered so far. This is his formulation of the classical general equilibrium model. This is the most advanced statement yet of the classical theory of value. The basic explanatory principles are the interdependence of physical production processes and the modifications introduced by capitalist production relations. It is the vision of interdependence which interests us here. Of course, this is the essence of any notion of general equilibrium, but Sraffa's is distinctly different from the neoclassical brand of general equilibrium analysis. While neoclassical analysis recognizes interdependence by making both supply and demand functions of all prices, Sraffa's analysis is so different he refuses even to use the terms "supply" and "demand."[7] For Sraffa, interdependence is a technical phenomenon arising from the nature of the production system itself. In particular, for the basic system, it is the fact of commodities which are their own means of production which forms the network of interdependence which allows Sraffa to have a determinate system (until labor shares in the surplus).

It is this feature which has led Brahmananda and Sraffa to
characterize it as picturing

> the system of production and consumption as a circular
> process [which] stands in striking contrast to the view
> presented by modern theory, of a one-way avenue that leads
> from 'Factors of production' to 'Consumption goods'.[8]

Therefore, Sraffa goes to great lengths to avoid words such as
"factors of production," "costs of production," and "supply and
demand" because they have no meaning independent of the results
of the solutions for prices and distribution, and because "cost
of production" for a basic product depends as much on the price
of the product itself as does the price of the product depend
on the "cost of production." This terminology

> would be adequate so far as non-basic products were
> concerned, since . . . their exchange-ratio is merely a
> reflection of what must be paid for means of production,
> labour and profits in order to produce them--there is no
> mutual dependence.
>
> But for a basic product there is another aspect to be
> considered. Its exchange-ratio depends as much on the use
> that is made of it in the production of other basic
> commodities as on the extent to which those commodities
> enter its own means of production. (One might be tempted,
> but it would be misleading, to say that 'it depends as
> much on the Demand side as on the Supply side.')[9]

Furthermore, Sraffa applies the notion of commodities
producing themselves to value and distribution. In the case of
value the solution depends on inputs and outputs being the same.
In the case of distribution, this idea is the kernel of the
surplus theory of profit of Marx and Ricardo, and it is the
starting point of Sraffa's theory. When we consider the title
of his book, it would appear we are correct in arguing this

idea is the key to the analysis.

We can now draw three important corollaries. First, this vision of Sraffa's does away with some basic confusions in Ricardo's work which have been a constant source of misunderstanding in the history of economics. This is Ricardo's usage of the term "cost of production." Several times in the "Notes on Malthus" and other places Ricardo argued cost of production, not supply and demand, was the ultimate cause of value.[10] This has led to interpretations which place Ricardo in the same tradition with Mill and Marshall, and has led to Schumpeter's accusation Ricardo was blind to the role of supply and demand in his own theory of value.[11] We can now see that it is possible to remain within the Ricardian tradition without resort to "cost of production" explanation, and that, therefore, Sraffa's system undercuts this view of history.

Second, the labor theory of value, insofar as it attempts to explain relative prices, is a special case of Sraffa's commodities theory. They both are based on a similar view of value as a social relation reflecting a physical relation, and they can both be expressed in general equilibrium terms. However, they give the same results only when profits are zero or when the proportions of labor and means of production are the same in all industries, i.e. only when labor values correspond to competitive market prices.

Third, since Sraffa's view of interdependence renders demand superfluous within the basic sector, the whole issue of constant versus increasing or decreasing returns to scale becomes a dead letter. This is partly because changes in scale and proportions of factors is ruled out from the beginning,[12] and partly because the relative price structure can change only if the whole technical structure of production is changed. Returns to scale only enter the determination, over time, of the proportion of total output which is surplus.

In summary, Sraffa has made several important contributions to be classical tradition, all of which hinge on his central conception of the basic sector being composed of a group of commodities which are their own means of production. He has solved the problem of the standard of value, the transformation problem, and the problem of operationalizing and generalizing the labor theory. More importantly, he has conceived a system of a well proportioned economy wherein his central concept serves as the starting point for value and distribution theory. In so doing, he has cast out such terms as "factors of production," "cost of production," and "supply and demand" which are integral features of an entirely different vision. These terms exist in the classical tradition only in early and sometimes confused work. Bearing in mind our earlier discussion, we feel secure in claiming there has been definite improvement in the classical analysis.

THE DEVELOPMENT OF ECONOMICS: THE RELATION OF CLASSICAL TO NEOCLASSICAL ECONOMICS

We have alluded to an interpretation of the history of
economic thought which seems to be very prevalent and which
this analysis of the classical tradition shows to be inadequate. The above reference to Ricardo's usage of the term
"cost of production" brought out a basic confusion in the
classical analysis which has led to the interpretation of the
history of economics in which neoclassical economics is an
evolution from the more primitive classical theory. On this
interpretation, the neoclassical theory from Marshall onwards
is a generalization and simplification of the classical theory
in which change in approach is conceived as the key difference,
rather than change in the fundamental vision of economic
society. The interpretation derives from Marshall in his
appendix on Ricardo where he hints that his theory generalizes
Ricardo's because Ricardo took the case of constant returns to
be typical of most commodities.[13] Subsequently variations of
this theme are found in many of the most respected works on
the history of economic thought. Blaug for example states:

> As a theory of relative prices, . . . the labor theory of
> value is nothing but a static theory of general equilib-
> rium, applicable to any closed exchange economy regardless
> of the character of property ownership, provided the input
> coefficients of production are given by technical consid-
> erations and perfect competition prevails. The labor
> theory is a special case of the more general Walrasian
> theory.[14]

Schumpeter seems to be closer to understanding neoclassical

theory as a complete shift in the underlying vision, but he does not seem to actually penetrate beyond the conventional view.

> The replacement of the geocentric by the heliocentric system and the replacement of the 'classic' by the marginal utility system were performances of the same kind: they were both essentially simplifying and unifying reconstructions.[15]

This type of interpretation frequently focuses on two alleged lines of continuity between the two traditions. These are Marshall's emphasis on 'real cost' as the long run determinant of value, and the development of the marginal productivity theory as a generalization of Ricardo's theory of rent. By incorporating the classical emphasis on cost, Marshall is said to have "reaffirmed" and "extended"[16] the classical tradition, and produced a theory of value which is formally identical to the classical labor theory in the case of constant returns to scale.[17] Similarly, in spite of Wicksteed's assertion that Ricardo's idea of marginal increments is substantially different,[18] the marginal productivity theory became a generalization of the Ricardian theory of rent.[19] By applying the marginal principle to all factors, rent is merely the marginal productivity of land which appears as a surplus simply because land assumes the role of the fixed factor. Likewise, the exploitation of labor by capital disappears when labor, not capital, is fixed while capital varies in quantity. As a result the whole concept of surplus becomes a peculiarity of which factor is being held fixed. What appears as a surplus is in

fact some factor's marginal product since in perfect competition the sum of marginal products times quantities exactly
exhausts the total product. It is the extension of the marginal principle which gives neoclassical theory its superior-
ity because it can unify the determination of factor shares
under one idea.[20] In fact, some commentators have considered
marginalism and the questions to which it lends itself the
basic distinction between the two traditions.

> The significance of marginal-utility theory was that it
> provided the archtype of the general problem of allocat-
> ing given means with maximum effect. It was not long
> before the same approach was extended from the household
> to the firm, from the theory of consumption to the theory
> of production. The theory of utility supplied most of
> the excitement of discovery in the seventies and eighties,
> but it was the introduction of marginal analysis as such
> that marked the true dividing line between classical
> theory and modern economics.[21]

These interpretations of the history of economics seem to
fall into the teleological approach discussed above in
Chapter 2. Classical theory is conceived as an embryo of
modern theory. Little, if any, consideration is given to the
possibility that the basic difference between the two traditions
is one of vision rather than change of emphasis or generalization within the same vision. Coats summarizes this view best:

> economics may be regarded as more 'uniformitarian' than
> the natural sciences, for despite persistent and often
> penetrating criticism by a stream of heterodox writers. . .
> it has been dominated throughout its history by a simple
> paradigm--the theory of economic equilibrium via the
> market mechanism.[22]

In opposition to this there is emerging a new interpretation
of the history of economics which focuses on the difference

110

between classical and neoclassical economics as being fundamentally a difference of <u>vision</u>. This view seeks to portray classical theory based on a different conception of the fundamental shape of economic society and hence, a different conception of the lines of causation within the system. This idea has received a major inpetus from the famous re-switching and quantity-of-capital debates in recent years.[23]

Viewing Sraffa as a rehabilitation of the earlier classical analysis, Dobb and Meek have begun to lay the ground work for a new approach to the history of economics. In a recent article Meek has concentrated on the re-emergence of classical-type analysis as proof that the Schumpeterian idea that classical analysis is a detour in the sweep of history is wrong:

> it seems to me that in the light of the 'Sraffa revolution' of the 1960's, the Ricardian-Marxian analysis can no longer be plausibly considered by anyone as having been a mere 'detour.'[24]

Far from being a detour

> Ricardo and Marx (and their progenitors) were the founders of a long tradition which has stretched, through the Marxian 'transformation problem' debates, Sraffa's commodity-production models, and the so-called neo-Ricardianism of the 1960's, right down to our own time. The basic idea which all those who have worked within this tradition have had in common is that the explanatory principle employed in value analysis should be firmly and more or less exclusively anchored to man's activity and relationships <u>as a producer</u>.[25]

Perhaps more than any one individual Maurice Dobb is responsible for the initial impetus of this interpretation beginning in some of his early essays on classical political

111

economy where he concentrates on the similarities between classical and Marxian theory in opposition to the modern subjective theory,[26] through his comments on Sraffa and the re-switching debates, which again focus on the similarity between this and the Marxian transformation problem,[27] and finally culminating in his recent book in which the grand theme of economic thought dominated by two distinct traditions emerges as the central theme:

> it is clear that there were, broadly speaking, two quite distinct and rival traditions in nineteenth-century economic thought as to the order and mode of determination of phenomena of exchange and income distribution. One of these deriving from Adam Smith treated the value of any commodity as being determined as the sum of the various expenses or costs involved in its production . . . . Determination of these necessary payments was viewed in a general supply-and-demand framework.[28]

Later economists than Ricardo such as Senior and Longfield developed this into the cost of production theory in which cost is a subjective factor used to explain wages and profits. "As such it descended through John Stuart Mill (though incongruously sailing under the flag of Ricardo) to Alfred Marshall."[29] Later versions of this allegedly post-Ricardian tradition, laying strong emphasis on demand, focused on another essential feature of this approach. The theoretical framework laid determination entirely within the sphere of exchange on the market, with the corollary that such institutional considerations as property ownership and social class were irrelevant.[30]

This stands in stark contrast to the other tradition which we have taken pains to develop in this book. This tradition also derives from Smith through Ricardo's theory of value which made the conditions of production the ultimate determinant of value in pre-capitalist and capitalist societies. This tradition thus, "rejected the possibility of treating the sphere of exchange-relations as an 'isolated system'."[31] The production process was prior to and dominated exchange processes. Furthermore, the social relations of production were introduced as an institutional datum determining the outcome of distribution prior to exchange taking place.

This book has been designed as a specialized treatise on the classical tradition to serve as an elaboration on and extension of this new view of the history of economic thought. By providing a clear exposition of the classical approach, uncluttered with discussions of simultaneous developments within the "market" tradition, we have focused more clearly than any single author to date on the historical continuity from Smith to Sraffa. The transformation problem debates were viewed as a detour since with Dmitriev and Sraffa it becomes superflous, and the labor theory of value is considered a special case of the Sraffa system rather than as a special case of the Walrasian system. This is not the place to launch a full scale rewriting of the history of economic thought. However, when such an undertaking is attempted on a grand scale, it appears that the dual development of these alternative traditions, along with the neoclassical "vice" of consistently misinterpreting the classical school would occupy center stage. The result would be a history in opposition to the type of history which itself derived from this persistent lack of understanding which derives from fundamentally different visions of reality. That is really not history at all, since by removing discontinuities and revolutionary changes from the sweep of development, the lessons of history and, hence, the present meaning of history, is lost. Rather it

> is merely the effect of the retrospective illusion of a given historical result which writes its history in the 'future anterior,' and which therefore thinks its origin as the anticipation of its end.[32]

BEYOND HISTORY: INTERSECTION WITH THE SOCIAL SCENE

Economic theory has developed as a means to influence social policy and the direction of human development itself. It is not merely abstract game-playing. Theoretical work acquires meaning and becomes worthwhile only if it intersects with the social scene of the times.[33] Our analysis of classical economics does so on two levels; the moral and the analytical.

On the moral level the main purpose of this work has been to achieve dialogue between the competing schools of thought. Recognizing that at bottom differences in vision are a complex mixture of differences in perception and in social values, we must conclude visions cannot really be translated. Rather it is necessary to understand the basic propositions of

traditions in order to achieve dialogue. Also, since these
basic propositions are in some sense scientific, it may be
possible to use science as an avenue toward settling values
differences. This is significant because, in the absence of
scientific reason, values conflicts can only be solved through
the use of force. This is the only logical answer to a situation where values conflicts must be solved, but the use of
reason has been ruled out as a means to solving them. This is
the end result of a view of science which sees a strict
dichotomy between science and values. In our conception of
economic theory as bearing a close relation to social values
and social issues, economic theory is an aid to human improvement, and is a branch of the science of value.

On the analytical level, the rehabilitation of the classical theory of value offers a fresh approach to several
important questions. For example, Professor Zinke has applied
Sraffa's system of price determination to the problems of
national economic planning.[34] Sraffa's production equations
are the key to determining prices within the basic sector
which will allow for a perfectly proportioned system, and the
linear relation between wages and profits allows the setting
of the rate of accumulation once the wage is specified. This
latter decision is made exogenously on the basis of what
society wants. This possibility of determining distribution
exogenously and without disturbing the production system is the
result of the indeterminacy of Sraffa's system when the wage is

part of the surplus. There is room for an infinite number of income distributions to exist with a given production system. As long as a surplus exists, human welfare does not have to be subservient to economic "necessity," a rise in wages would not throw the whole system out of proportion. Furthermore, the mix of a final output is a social decision as well. These decisions imply a set of prices which will keep the system proportioned. Thus, prices are set on the basis of social priorities, not vice versa.

Another area where classical analysis might be fruitfully applied is the whole range of questions surrounding long run economic growth, resource constraints, and environmental decay. These are the modern version of the classical concern for development, population, and diminishing returns. For example, we might consider the classical idea of the falling rate of profit as the same as the falling rate of surplus production, R, in a physical sense. If we could determine this as a real trend, we might shed valuable light on the future of economic growth.

Furthermore, the broadening of the subject matter of economics to include social relations would once again bring the problem of viable institutions into the forefront of economic thought. A conception of this type could not help but to structure thought toward the welfare implications not only of the exchange process but of the institutions themselves. Hence, the social structure of society would, from the logic of the vision itself be treated as variable rather than as constant.

These are a few of the ways in which the revitalization of classical theory may be beneficial. To date its role has been primarily negative, as a critique of generally accepted theory, but, if the debates touched off by Sraffa's rehabilitation are to lead to progress, it will be necessary for the disputants to move in the direction outlined in this study. The real battle field is the theory of value and values, and this has not been entered. Blame must lie with both sides in this matter. It lies on the side of the neoclassical economists for refusing to understand the opposition and for clinging to a discredited theory of value. It lies with the new-classical economists for emphasizing the strength of their view as being a critique, rather than as a positive approach to economic problems in its own right. We have attempted to correct for this latter **failing** by laying the groundwork for classical theory to once more flourish as a viable approach to social-economic problems rather than as a detour in the sweep of history.

117

1. This idea is a bit tricky because many writers have put forth solutions to old problems by knowingly or not, changing the problem. For example, the Ricardian problem of the effect of unequal proportions of fixed capital on equilibrium prices is "solved" by the marginal theory by making capital productive of value because it imparts greater utility to the total product via the productivity of roundabout methods of production. However, this is not Ricardo's problem at all. Ricardo's problem arose out of a vision which linked value to physical relations within the production process. But, since distribution between productive classes affected the formation of equilibrium values, the correspondence was not direct, hence the search for an invariant standard of value. The marginalist answer, using classical terminology, describes the role of capital in the creation of wealth not value. Furthermore, in the neoclassical system the effects of distribution on prices is mainly via its effects on consumer demand, rather than via its effects on the prices of production of commodities.

2. This last aspect of progress is the same as Schumpeter's. It seems fairly straight-forward since the world is in fact interdependent that, therefore, ideas which capture this are better than those which do not.

3. The question of the relation of Sraffa to Marxian economics is currently a topic of considerable debate among Marxists. Meek, Dobb, and Eatwell defend Sraffa as having solved some important technical problems in the Marxian theory of value, and as having placed social relations of production back into the heart of economic analysis. Lebowitz and Rowthorn commend Sraffa for attacking the neoclassical theory, but argue that he is essentially Ricardian rather than Marxian. To them, this means he derives value from technical, not social, relations; he is ahistorical in the sense that capitalism appears as a fixed, eternal system rather than as a passing state; and he fails to explain the origin of profits. From what we have said in Chapters 1 through 4 there should be little doubt we do not sympathize with this view. Sraffa's theory is not incompatible with Marx's nor is it incompatible with Marx's emphasis on social relations of production.

4. D. M. Nuti, Introduction to V. K. Dmitriev: Economic Essays, p. 17. Although Sraffa must share this distinction with Dmitriev, it is appropriate to emphasize it as one of his contributions because there has been a great deal of debate and time spent on the correct solution since Dmitriev wrote. It seems the classical tradition has the same problem as the neoclassical in having to periodically rediscover ideas of forgotten forerunners.

5. William J. Baumol, "The Transformation of Values: What Marx, 'Really' Meant (An Interpretation)," Journal of Economic Literature 12 (1, 1964): 51-62.

6. Eatwell, "Controversies in the Theory of Surplus Value."

7. Sraffa, Production of Commodities, p. 9.

8. Ibid., p. 93. See also P. R. Brahmananda, The New-Classical Versus the Neo-Classical Economics, p. xxiv, and Edward Nell, "Economics: The Revival of Political Economy," in Ideology and Social Science, edited by Robin Blackburn, (New York: Random House, 1972), pp. 76-95.

9. Sraffa, Production of Commodities, pp. 8-9.

10. David Ricardo, "Notes on Malthus," Works and Correspondence, Vol. 2, p. 40.

11. Schumpeter, History of Economic Analysis, p. 601.

12. Sraffa, Production of Commodities, p. v.

13. Marshall, Principles of Economics, p. 814.

14. Blaug, Economic Theory in Retrospect, p. 271.

15. Schumpeter, History of Economic Analysis, p. 919.

16. Everett Johnson Burtt, Jr., Social Perspectives in the History of Economic Theory, (New York: St. Martin's Press, 1972), p. 201.

17. E. K. Hunt and Howard Sherman, "Value, Alienation, and Distribution," Science and Society 36 (1, 1972): 34.

18. Phillip H. Wicksteed, "The Scope and Method of Political Economy in the Light of the 'Marginal' Theory of Value and Distribution," Economic Journal 34 (1914): 18-20. Although arguing in favor of the marginal productivity theory, Wicksteed takes special pains to point out that the marginal theory rests on taking homogenous doses of the variable factor in order to determine a functional relation between quantity and productivity. The Ricardian theory rests on taking heterogeneous units of land. No functional relation is established. The former gives rise to rent as a peculiarity of a fixed factor, while the latter focuses on the peculiarities of land itself.

19. Martin Bronfenbrenner, Income Distribution Theory, (Chicago: Aldine, Atherton, Inc., 1971), p. 172.

20. S. N. Alam, "The Marginal Productivity Theory: A Survey," Indian Economic Journal 18 (2, 1970): 238.

21. Blaug, Economic Theory in Retrospect, p. 299. See also Donald Winch, "Marginalism and the Boundaries of Economic Science," in Black et al, Marginal Revolution, pp. 61-62. Winch argues marginalism changed the focus of economics to scarcity and allocation.

22. A. W. Coats, "Is There a Structure of Scientific Revolutions in Economics?" Kyklos 22 (2, 1969): 292.

23. See Harcourt, Some Cambridge Controversies in the Theory of Capital. At issue was the general validity of the marginal productivity theory. The Cambridge England school demonstrated the impossibility of equating the rate of profits to the marginal productivity of capital when capital-labor ratios varied between techniques. The result was that a single "quantity of capital" per worker was not uniquely associated with one rate of profit.

24. Meek, "Value in the History of Economic Thought," p. 248.

25. Ibid., p. 250.

26. Dobb, Political Economy and Capitalism, ch. 1-3.

27. Dobb, "The Sraffa System and Critique of the Neo-Classical Theory of Distribution."

28. Dobb, Theories of Value and Distribution, p. 112.

29. Ibid., p. 113.

30. Ibid., pp. 113-114.

31. Ibid., p. 115.

32. Althusser, Reading Capital, p. 44.

33. Leo Rogin, The Meaning and Validity of Economic Theory, pp. 1-13.

34. George W. Zinke, The Book of Priorities: A Treatise on Moral Economics, unpublished manuscript.

Bibliography

Alam, S. N. "The Marginal Productivity Theory: A Survey."
Indian Economic Journal 18 (1970): 230-249.

Althusser, Louis, and Balibar, Etienne. Reading Capital.
New York: Pantheon Books, 1970.

American Economic Association. Readings in the Theory of
Income Distribution. Philadelphia: Blakiston, 1946.

Bajt, A. "Labour as Scarcity in Marx's Value Theory: An
Alternative Interpretation." History of Political Economy
3 (1971): 152-169.

Baumol, William J. "The Transformation of Values: What Marx
'Really' Meant (An Intrepretation)." Journal of Economic
Literature 12 (1974): 51-62.

Black, R. D. Collison, et al, eds. The Marginal Revolution
in Economics. Durham, North Carolina: Duke University Press,
1973.

Blackburn, Robin, ed. Ideology and Social Science. New York:
Random House, 1972.

Blaug, Mark. Economic Theory in Retrospect. 2d rev. ed.
Homewood, Illinois: Richard D. Irwin, Inc., 1968.

Bortkiewicz, L. V. "Value and Price in the Marxian System,"
reprinted in International Economic Papers No. 2 (1952):
5-60.

Bose, Arun. "The 'Labour Approach' and the 'Commodity Approach'
in Mr. Sraffa's Price Theory." Economic Journal 74 (1964):
722-726.

_____. "Marx on Value, Capital, and Exploitation."
History of Political Economy 3 (1971): 298-334.

Boulding, Kenneth E. "After Samuelson Who Needs Adam Smith?"
History of Political Economy 3 (1971): 225-237.

Brahmananda, P. R. "The Economics of Paul Anthony Samuelson."
Indian Economic Journal 18 (1970): 251-269.

_____. The New-Classical Versus the Neo-Classical
Economics. Mysore: Prasarange University of Mysore, 1967.

Bronfenbrenner, Martin. Income Distribution Theory. Chicago:
Aldine, Atherton, Inc., 1971.

Burtt, Everett Johnson, Jr. Social Perspectives in the History of Economic Theory. New York: St. Martin's Press, 1972.

Cassels, J. M. "A Re-Interpretation of Ricardo on Value." Quarterly Journal of Economics, 49 (1935): 518-532.

Clifton, James A. "Competition and the Evolution of the Capitalist Made of Production." Cambridge Economic Journal 1 (1977): 137-151.

Coats, A. W. "Is There a Structure of Scientific Revolutions in Economics?" Kyklos 22 (1969): 289-296.

Collard, D. A. "The Production of Commodities." Economic Journal, 73 (1963): 144-146.

_____. "Rejoinder." Economic Journal 74 (1964): 726-727.

Dietz, James L. "Paradise Reswitched." Review of Radical Political Economy 5 (1973): 1-17.

Dobb, Maurice. Political Economy and Capitalism: Some Essays in Economic Tradition. London: Routledge & Kegan Paul, Ltd., 1972.

_____. Theories of Value and Distribution Since Adam Smith: Ideology and Economic Theory. Cambridge: Cambridge University Press, 1973.

_____, "'Vulgar Economics' and 'Vulgar Marxism': A Reply." Journal of Political Economy 48 (1940): 251-258.

Eatwell, John. "Controversies in the Theory of Surplus Value: Old and New." Science and Society 38 (1974): 281-303.

_____. "Mr. Sraffa's Standard Commodity and the Rate of Exploitation." Quarterly Journal of Economics 89 (1975): 543-555.

Engels, Frederick. Preface to Capital, Vol. 2. Moscow: Progress Publishers.

Friedman, Milton. "The Methodology of Positive Economics," in Readings in Microeconomics, edited by William Breit and Harold M. Hochman, 2d. ed. New York: Holt, Rinehart and Winston, Inc., 1968.

Godelier, Maurice. Rationality and Irrationality in Economics. New York: Monthly Review Press, 1972.

Gordon, Donald F. "What was the Labor Theory of Value?"
    American Economic Review: Papers and Proceedings 49 (1959):
    462-472.

Harrod, Roy F. "Review of Sraffa." Economic Journal 71
    (1961): 783-787.

Harcourt,G. C. Some Cambridge Controversies in the Theory of
    Capital. Cambridge: Cambridge University Press, 1972.

Horowitz, David, ed. Marx and Modern Economics. New York:
    Monthly Review Press, 1969.

Horvat, Branko. Towards a Theory of Planned Economy. Belgrade:
    Yugoslav Institute of Economic Research, 1964.

Hunt, E. K. "Religious Parable Versus Economic Logic."
    Intermountain Economic Review 2 (1971): 1-14.

Hunt, E. K. and Sherman, Howard. "Value, Alienation, and
    Distribution." Science and Society 36 (1972): 29-48.

Hunt, E. K., and Schwartz, Jesse, eds. A Critique of Economic
    Theory. Harmondsworth, Middlesex, England: Penguin Books,
    Ltd., 1972.

Hutchison, T. W. "Some Questions about Ricardo." Economica 19
    (1952): 415-432.

Kaldor, Nicholas. "Alternative Theories of Distribution," in
    Essays on Value and Distribution. London: Gerald Duckworth
    & Co., Ltd., 1960.

Kauder, Emil. A History of Marginal Utility Theory. Princeton:
    Princeton University Press, 1965.

Knight, Frank. "The Ricardian Theory of Production and Dis-
    tribution." The Canadian Journal of Economics and Political
    Science 1 (1935): 3-25, 171-196.

Kuhn, Thomas S. The Structure of Scientific Revolutions,
    2d ed. Chicago: The University of Chicago Press, 1970.

Lebowitz, Michael. "The Crisis of Economic Theory." Science
    and Society 37 (1973-1974): 63-87.

Lerner, A. P. "From Vulgar Economy to Vulgar Marxism."
    Journal of Political Economy 47 (1939): 557-567.

_____. "A Further Note." Journal of Political Economy 48
    (1940): 258-260.

Levine, A. L. "This Age of Leontief . . . and Who? An
Interpretation." Journal of Economic Literature 12 (1974):
872-881.

Lukacs, Georg. History and Class Consciousness, New Edition.
Cambridge: Massachusetts, MIT Press, 1971.

Macfie. Alec L. An Essay on Economy and Value. London:
Macmillan & Co., Ltd., 1936.

Marshall, Alfred. Principles of Economics: An Introductory
Volume, 8th Ed. New York: The Macmillan Co., 1948.

Marx, Karl. Capital, 3rd ed. Moscow: Progress Publishers.

Mattick, Paul. "Samuelson's 'Transformation' of Marxism into
Bourgeois Economics." Science and Society 36 (1972):
258-273.

May, Kenneth. "The Structure of Classical Value Theory."
Review of Economic Studies 17 (1949-1950): 60-69.

Meek, Ronald. "The Decline of Ricardian Economics in England."
Economica 17 (1950): 43-62.

_____. Economics and Ideology and Other Essays. London:
Chapman & Hall, Ltd., 1967.

_____, Smith, Marx, and After. London: Chapman & Hall,
Ltd., 1977.

_____. Studies in the Labour Theory of Value. 2d ed.
London: Lawrence and Wishart, 1973.

_____. "Value in the History of Economics." History of
Political Economy 6 (1974): 246-260.

Mill, John Stuart. Principles of Political Economy: With Some
of Their Applications to Social Philosophy. New York:
A. M. Kelley, 1965.

Morishima, Michio. Marx's Economics, A Dual Theory of Value
and Growth. Cambridge: Cambridge University Press, 1973.

Morris, Jacob. "Some Comments on Marx's Theory of Value."
Science and Society 6 (1972): 341-343.

Minsky, Hyman P. John Maynard Keynes. New York: Columbia
University Press, 1975.

Myint, Hla. Theories of Welfare Economics. Cambridge, Massachusetts: Harvard University Press, 1948.

Myrdal, Gunnar. The Political Element in the Development of Economic Thought. Cambridge, Massachusetts: Harvard University Press, 1955.

Nuti, Domenico, M., ed. V. K. Dmitriev: Economic Essays on Value, Competition and Utility. Cambridge: Cambridge University Press, 1974.

Quandt, Richard E. "Review of Sraffa." Journal of Political Economy 69 (1961): 500.

Rauner, Robert W. Samuel Bailey and the Classical Theory of Value. Cambridge, Massachusetts: Harvard University Press, 1961.

Reder, Melvin W. "Review." American Economic Review 51 (1961): 688-695.

Ricardo, David. The Works and Correspondence of David Ricardo, edited by Piero Sraffa. Cambridge: Cambridge University Press, 1951.

Roberts, Paul C. and Stephenson, Mathew A. Marx's Theory of Exchange, Alienation and Crises. Stanford: Hoover Institution Press, 1973.

Robertson, D., Shove, G..F., and Sraffa, P. "Increasing Returns and the Representative Firm: A symposium," Economic Journal, 40 (1930): 79-116.

Robinson, Joan. Collected Economic Papers, Vols. 2, 3, 4. Oxford: Basil Blackwell, 1964, 1965, 1973, resp.

_____. Economic Philosophy. Garden City, New York: Doubleday Inc., 1964.

_____. An Essay on Marxian Economics. London: Macmillan Press, Ltd., 1972.

_____. "Piero Sraffa and the Rate of Exploitation." New Left Review 31 (1965): 28-34.

Rogin, Leo. The Meaning and Validity of Economic Theory. New York: Harper and Brothers, 1956.

Roosevelt, Frank. "Controversies in Economic Theory Cambridge Economics as Commodity Fetishism. Review of Radical Political Economics 7 (1975): 1-32.

Rowthorn, Bob. "Neo-Classicism, Neo-Ricardianism, and Marxism."
New Left Review 86 (1974): 63-87.

Rubin, Isaak Illich. Essays on Marx's Theory of Value.
Detroit: Black and Red, 1972.

Samuelson, Paul A. Economics. 8th ed. New York: McGraw-Hill
Book Company, 1970.

Sastri, K. V. S. "The Ricardian Theory of Factor Shares."
Explorations in Economic History 8 (1971): 425-444.

Schumpeter, Joseph A. History of Economic Analysis. New York:
Oxford University Press, 1968.

Sraffa, Piero. "The Laws of Returns Under Competitive
Conditions." Economic Journal 36 (1926): 535-550.

_____. Production of Commodities by Means of Commodities:
Prelude to a Critique of Economic Theory. Cambridge:
Cambridge University Press, 1960.

_____. "Production of Commodities: a Comment." Economic
Journal 72 (1962): 477-479.

Smith Adam. An Inquiry into the Nature and Causes of the Wealth
of Nations, edited by Edwin Cannan. New York: Random
House, Inc., 1937.

Stephenson, Mathew A. "The Paradox of Value: A Suggested
Interpretation." History of Political Economy 4 (1972):
127-139.

Stigler, George J. Essays in the History of Economics.
Chicago: University of Chicago Press, 1965.

Sweezy, Paul M. The Theory of Capitalist Development:
Principles of Marxian Political Economy. New York: Monthly
Review Press, 1942.

Townsend, Harry, ed. Price Theory. Harmondsworth, Middlesex,
England: Penguin Books, Ltd., 1973.

Tucker, G. S. L. "The Origin of Ricardo's Theory of Profit."
Economica 21 (1954): 320-333.

University of Chicago Department of Political Economy. Outlines
of Economics, Developed in a Series of Problems. Chicago:
University of Chicago Press, 1914.

Walras, Leon. Elements of Pure Economics, 4th ed. London: Allen & Unwin, Ltd., 1954.

Ward, Benjamin. What's Wrong with Economics? New York: Basic Books, 1972.

Weizsacker, C. C. von. "Morishima on Marx." Economic Journal 83 (1973): 1245-1254.

Wicksell, Knut. Value, Capital, and Rent. London: George Allen & Unwin, Ltd., 1954.

Wicksteed, Phillip H. The Common Sense of Political Economy. London: George Routledge & Sons, Ltd., 1945.

_____. "The Scope and Method of Political Economy in the Light of the 'Marginal' Theory of Value and Distribution." Economic Journal 24 (1914): 1-23.

Wieser, Friedrich Von. Natural Value. New York: Kelley & Millman, 1956.

Winternitz, J. "Values and Prices: A Solution of the So-Called Transformation Problem." Economic Journal 58 (1948): 276-280.

Wong, Stanley. "The 'F-Twist' and the Methodology of Paul Samuelson." American Economic Review 63 (1973): 312-325.

Zinke, George W. The Book of Priorities: A Treatise on Moral Economics. unpublished manuscript.

Zinke, George W. The Problem of Malthus: Must Progress End in Overpopulation?, University of Colorado Studies/Series in Economics, No. 5. Boulder: University of Colorado Press, 1967.